FEMINISM, CULTURE AND POLITICS

FEMINISM, CULTURE AND POLITICS

edited by

Rosalind Brunt
and
Caroline Rowan

LAWRENCE AND WISHART
LONDON

Lawrence and Wishart Limited
39 Museum Street
London WC1A 1LQ

First published 1982
© Lawrence and Wishart, 1982

Photoset in North Wales by
Derek Doyle & Associates, Mold, Clwyd.
Printed in Great Britain by
Camelot Press, Southampton

Contents

List of Illustrations

Acknowledgements

We are grateful to Judy Chicago for her kind permission to use photographs of *The Dinner Party*, and to Jill Posener for kind permission to use her two photographs.

Introduction

The Women's Liberation Movement has always been a disruptive element and a major target of its disruptive behaviour has been the dominant culture. From the disruption of the 'Miss World Contest', through our spray-painting of adverts and cinema screens and our 'Reclaim The Night' demonstrations, to the proliferation of feminist theatre groups and film distributors, and our struggles for access to the mass media, the women's movement has not let up in its attack on male-defined culture.

These disruptive events were and continue to be important, because they challenge the taken-for-granted. By disturbing and subverting common-sense stereotypes which oppress women, we are proving that our subordination is socially constructed. It is not natural or biological.

Feminist cultural politics takes many forms. Direct action, for example, makes visible that which was previously unnoticed. When women on 'Reclaim the Night' demonstrations take over the streets, invading the territory of male predators, they are both celebrating the solidarity of women and forcefully drawing attention to the generally invisible barriers which make those streets no-go areas for women.

Another major form of feminist cultural politics is the construction of alternatives. This involves not only changes in the cultural 'product', like books, films and theatre, but more importantly, the establishment of different ways of working.

Feminists are attempting to develop more democratic practices – such as collective decision-making and active participation through small groups and workshops.

These examples illustrate the way in which feminism had broadened and transformed the definition of what is political. Both norms of political behaviour (from forms of address to the representation of women on decision-making bodies), and the range of issues considered legitimate areas of political struggle, have been substantially influenced by the women's movement.

An important aspect of this transformative process has been the development of women's studies and the invasion by feminism of traditional academic disciplines. Those involved in women's studies insist that knowledge be made more accessible and more politically relevant. At the same time, women's studies aims to transform the boundaries of knowledge, by offering a critique which highlights the absences and silences of orthodox approaches. It is vital that women's studies maintains its close links with the Women's Liberation Movement. Otherwise, it risks slipping into orthodoxy and academic elitism.

It is in this context that we have edited a book about cultural politics. Following the women's movement's definitions, we have used the term 'culture' in its broadest sense, to include the experiences of everyday life: the family, sexuality and ageing and also in its 'documentary' sense, choosing cultural products which have had a formative influence on women's experience fictional and non-fictional bestsellers, advertisements and other visual representations of women. In the historical articles we have tried to link the 'documentary' notion of culture with that of experience and to relate the work of women in politics – as makers of history – to their everyday lives and struggles a wives, mothers and workers. We have tried to ensure that all the articles are relevant to feminist political practice and have strategic focus.

For our failure to seek out black feminist culture, we have only our own racism to blame. It is a serious omission. Whit feminists are now beginning to realise the extent to whic racism has divided the women's movement, and we hope that given this recognition, our error will not be repeated.

Although this book is addressed primarily to those alread

involved in the women's movement, we hope that its readership will extend beyond committed feminists, to those women and men for whom it is perhaps unfamiliar territory, but who are prepared to work towards an alliance with the women's movement.

Rosalind Brunt
Caroline Rowan

Inverts and Experts: Radclyffe Hall and the Lesbian Identity

Sonja Ruehl

Radclyffe Hall published her explicitly lesbian novel, *The Well of Loneliness*, in 1928. It is a work of polemical fiction setting out her view that lesbianism is inborn, an 'inversion' of normal sexuality which ought to be tolerated by society because it cannot be helped. When it was published, the book was immediately denounced by the *Sunday Express* as an insidious moral poison and within six weeks it was being prosecuted for obscenity. The trial and surrounding publicity about the book put lesbianism on the map. A battle over competing definitions of lesbianism was engaged and, for the first time, the idea of 'the lesbian' as a specific identity and image was given wide public currency.

Radclyffe Hall's public stance was that she wrote as a lesbian herself and the reports photographs and cartoons of her in the press turned her into the paradigm of lesbianism in appearance and manner. Her notoriety was the greater because by this time she was already an established novelist and literary prize-winner. Her upper-class provenance and aura of exotic masculinity contributed to public interest in her as a notorious personality. Both she and her fictional heroine, Stephen, became points of reference for women who, in a time when landmarks were few, were struggling to make sense of their attraction to other women and to find a social identity by which to live.

What affected the way women were able to live and construe their lives was not simply that lesbianism could be talked about, but the way it could be talked about. And I want to examine how lesbianism came to be defined as a sexual identity. As press reaction of the time illustrated, lesbianism before 1928 had commonly been situated predominantly within a rhetoric of sin, if it was discussed at all. The sinful perspective had already been challenged from within a restricted medical discourse by 'sexologists' such as Havelock Ellis, who had established lesbianism as a medical-psychological category. Radclyffe Hall used Ellis's category but deployed it in a different kind of discourse, a literary and fictional one. This in itself, together with her own public identification as a lesbian, contributed to the beginning of a transformation of Ellis's category and a shift in the definition of lesbianism. The events surrounding her book and its trial enable us to see competing definitions of lesbianism within the discourses of science, fiction and the popular press.

Where scientific definitions are concerned, a strand of medical-psychological opinion in the nineteenth century had begun to develop the idea that people could actually be defined by their sexual 'natures' – that lesbians, say, could actually be thought of as a separate type of person. 'Sexology' had started to classify and differentiate aberrant forms of sexuality more minutely than the moral and religious language of sin had done and also to categorise these sexual aberrations in biological terms. Havelock Ellis was the most influential of 'sexologists' in England. His work on homosexuality, entitled *Sexual Inversion*, had been published in 1897. The book had been prosecuted and found 'obscene' under the same law from which Hall later suffered, and the remainder of his series, *Studies in the Psychology of Sex*, had to be published in America.

Ellis developed the category of 'congenital inversion' to describe homosexuality. He viewed it as neither sin nor sickness: what was inborn could not be helped nor passed on to others. Although he realised that a theory of innateness provided a basis for public tolerance of homosexuality he never actively campaigned on the issue. 'Congenital inversion' remained a definition restricted to scientific discourse until given wide publicity through *The Well of Loneliness*. In order to consider how Hall's categorisation of homosexuality relates to that of Ellis – and what its political consequences might be – I want to draw on the work of the French philosopher, Michel Foucault.

From Imprisoning Categories to Self-Definition

In *The History of Sexuality* Foucault argues the need to examine sexuality in terms of historically specific discourses and their methods of classification. He challenges the view that sexuality has a coherent, unitary existence, at one moment repressed, at another, liberated. In his view, any coherence sexual activities may have derives entirely from the concepts and definitions that organise our knowledge of them. When he examines the work of nineteenth century 'sexologists' like Ellis he notes how they create a 'medical-psychological discourse' whereby 'peripheral' sexualities, like homosexuality, are organised into a scientific taxonomy, or classification system. The categories created by the system, such as Ellis's 'inversion', are then interpreted as permanent attributes of individuals.

Furthermore, these categories do not merely compose a person's identity: they *are* what defines it. Thus, from being an undifferentiated sin or piece of behaviour, 'lesbian' comes to denote a particular *identity* and 'the lesbian' as a separate type of person is then an invention of nineteenth century science. Foucault goes on to argue that once sexuality is constructed as the 'key', the 'secret', to an individual's 'true nature' or 'inner being', these categories have a rigidifying effect, imprisoning individuals whose lives are administered under them.

The intention of this 'medical-psychological discourse' was to organise sexuality into a new field of scientific knowledge, bringing it within the range of rationality as an area to which rules could be applied. But in Foucault's perspective, to organise a new field of knowledge is also to organise a new set of power relations: power is granted to the definers – the experts and administrators of others' sexuality.

At the same time, the process of categorisation makes resistance to that power possible. Once a category like homosexuality has been set up and individuals have started to be defined by it, then the so-named 'homosexuals' may group under it and start to use it to speak for themselves. So, Foucault says, 'homosexuality began to speak on its own behalf ... often in the same vocabulary, using the same categories, by which it was medically disqualified'. He calls this process the development of a 'reverse discourse', and it is in these terms that I want to examine the work of Radclyffe Hall.

I am going to consider how, speaking herself from within the category 'invert' developed by Ellis, she was able to begin its transformation. Her militant stand, both as author and public personality, was to start a 'reverse discourse' towards *self-definition* by those oppressed under the category. Hall's intervention can be seen as a step in the process whereby women have firstly been able to group under a publicly-available 'lesbian' label and later gone on to demand the right to define that category themselves. That challenge has arisen in the political groupings of the gay movements of the 1970s and especially of the women's movement, where the 'right to a self-defined sexuality' for all women explicitly emerged as one of the demands of women's liberation. But to understand in retrospect what Hall's contribution to that process was, it is necessary to look first at the way Ellis's theory worked to construct the lesbian person.

Havelock Ellis and 'Congenital Inversion'

In his work on homosexuality. Havelock Ellis made a distinction between homosexuality as an innate and permanent state and as tempoary, acquired behaviour. The first he called sexual 'inversion', a fixed congenital characteristic expressing a person's 'true' sexual nature, the second, because not innate, a potential temptation and a vice.

Because of this logical separation, Ellis believed that someone who was a congenital invert would not necessarily exhibit it in homosexual behaviour – while someone who was not could be tempted into temporary indulgence. True inverts could decide not to engage in homosexual practices, could choose not to give any physical expression to their homosexual nature. This is the course of action taken by the majority of the six 'inverted' women whose case-histories Ellis discusses in *Sexual Inversion.* How then could their inversion be revealed in the first place? It is revealed as a characteristic of these individuals through introspection and the self-confession of their 'natures' to Ellis, who intersperses the histories with his comments.

Ellis attempts to discover a coherent set of physical distinguishing marks which infallibly characterise female inverts. His failure to do so he ascribes to a lack of adequate scientific knowledge. Because his concept of lesbianism is biological, he seems to suggest that a coherent set of distinguishing marks could in time be discovered by medical science. In this way, he directs attention towards a search for the *symptoms* of lesbianism. One consequence of his view is therefore that women are left to worry about whether they exhibit 'symptoms' of lesbianism or not. This is especially so when combined with his view that inversion could not definitely be distinguished until a woman was in her twenties.

It is clear from this description of the kind of symptoms Ellis was looking for that he expected the 'true invert' to be a 'masculine' woman, exhibiting an active sexuality which he thought of as 'male'. The object of the true invert's desire, on the other hand, he expected to be feminine. In line with his conception of heterosexual relations, a 'feminine' or responsive sexuality was required to mesh with the active 'male' sexuality of the invert. This raises the problem of whether the 'feminine' partner was herself a true 'invert' or not.

Ellis extricates himself from this problem by distinguishing a separate class of 'women who-respond-to-true-inverts'. It is an overlapping category, with elements of the heterosexual woman and of the congenital invert. This object of the true invert's desire will most probably be a womanly woman but, Ellis argues, one who is not quite attractive enough to appeal to the average man. He also tries to create distinctions between what appeals to 'inverts' and 'what appeals to men' in terms such as that inverts are more interested in beauty of figure and men in beauty of face. The clinching argument for Ellis is, however, that this category, though 'womanly', is not 'robust', not 'well adapted for child-bearing', so that even here a biological justification is called into play. By tying his view of 'inversion' to heterosexual procreative sex as the model from which it deviates Ellis thus evokes the image of 'sterility', and the whole lesbian relationship begins to seem a sterile imitation and thereby inferior.

This may be the reason why Ellis overcompensates for the sexual aberration of inverts by suggesting that it is outweighed by other excellent qualities which in fact have nothing to do with homosexuality. Though he wants to argue that inverts should be tolerated by society, his views suggest that inversion 'in itself' is not as worthy of respect as the 'norm' of heterosexuality and that lesbians have to win social acceptance by being a generally superior type of person. In addition to character and intellect, this might be through the countervailing power of social position and Ellis points to the social superiority of belonging to the upper classes as one way women might, as it were, 'get away with' lesbianism, in moral terms. There are hints in the case-studies that high-mindedness might require rising above physical gratifications: inverts could divert their thoughts 'into intellectual channels' or try to 'find a way of life in which there was as little sex of any kind as possible'.

When Radclyffe Hall comes to write *The Well of Loneliness*, it is clear that she writes within the parameters set up by Ellis. His notions of biological destiny, symptoms of inborn and irreducible difference, the 'masculine' invert and the 'feminine' love-object, are all, as I shall indicate, woven into her fictional and partly autobiographical plot. Moreover, she was keen to acquire Ellis's expert backing for her views. She got him to write the preface to the first edition of the book, recommending it in the light of his own theories:

> I have read *The Well of Loneliness* with great interest because – apart from its fine qualities as a novel – it possesses a notable psychological and social significance. So far as I know, it is the first English novel which presents, in a completely faithful and uncompromising form, one particular aspect of sexual life as it exists among us today. The relation of certain people – who, while different from their fellow human beings, are sometimes of the highest character and the finest aptitudes – to the often hostile society in which they move presents difficult and still unsolved problems. The poignant situations which thus arise are here set forth so vividly, and yet with such complete absence of offence, that we must place Radclyffe Hall's book on a high level of distinction.

In this preface Ellis thus tries to set the terms for a discussion of lesbianism as 'social problem' and to shift it away from ideas of sin or moral degeneracy.

In pleading for tolerance of lesbianism, Hall had considerable scope to use the affective potentialities of the novel to engage her readers' sympathies. More vividly than Ellis does in his medical discourse, she is able to point up the social consequences of a lesbian identity and to explore, not only sexual relationships, but those involving family and friends. By contrast, Ellis's method seems rather individualising of lesbianism, because he presents individuals' stories circumscribed within the format of separate case-histories interspersed with his comments. What Hall does in her novel is to highlight what is only implicit in his theorising: the 'sterility' of lesbian relationships, described with images of barrenness and unfruitful wombs, to evoke sympathy for the unsurmountable grief of the 'true invert'. But *The Well of Loneliness* is not simply an exemplification of Ellis's views in literary form, nor just more persuasive because able to deploy the rhetoric of fiction. While Hall's own definition of lesbianism remains closely tied to Ellis's category of inversion, her novel is a deliberate political intervention. Through it, she takes a militant stance on behalf of all 'inverts' *because she speaks as one herself*. She starts the process of the 'reverse discourse' by opening up a space for other lesbians to speak for themselves, and later, through the contemporary gay and women's movements, to challenge the definition of the category from 'within'.

The Well of Loneliness : Unfolding Lesbian Destiny

The novel is the story of Stephen Gordon, born a girl to her father's disappointment and christened Stephen by his (prescient) whim. The novel suggests the presence of distinguishing marks of inversion. From birth, it is said, Stephen is a little strange, a 'narrow-hipped, wide-shouldered' baby with 'brave hazel eyes that were so like her father's'. Her mother turns from her with intuitive distaste, while Stephen has an instinctive empathy with her father. She grows up liking boyish pursuits of a suitably aristocratic kind and explicitly wants to be a boy, playing at being 'the young Nelson'. Thus symptoms of 'congenital inversion' are clearly implied. They take the specific form of her being a sort of failed boy, a caricature of her father and a 'blemished, unworthy, maimed reproduction' of him.

The reader's sympathy is enlisted on behalf of this invert, as yet a child and 'innocent' in the sense of being both ignorant of, and not responsible for, her 'condition'. Her father grows concerned and starts to read books by a German sexologist in his library. By this means, the reader is let in on the 'truth'. The novel constructs Stephen's 'inversion' as containing the essence of her nature, a 'secret' hidden even from herself. She asks her father whether there is something strange about herself and although he is not quite man enough to share it with her, it is her father who holds the knowledge of Stephen's destiny.

The gradual unfolding of this biological destiny is traced through Stephen's amorous history. After a childish infatuation with a housemaid, one summer, in accordance with the dictates of her nature, she falls 'quite simply and naturally in love' with Angela, wife of a local businessman. Angela is only tempted onto the fringes of homosexuality by boredom and proves perfidious because, as it turns out, she also has a male lover. She embodies the 'viciousness' of acquired homosexuality which Ellis alludes to and a clear contrast with Stephen is established: she isn't even 'a lady'. Class is invoked on behalf of the invert.

The novel also presents Stephen with the possibility of an amorous encounter with a man, which it shows to be unworkable. Martin, a young man from the colonies, is used to boyishness in women and so doesn't find Stephen's manners strange. But she is puzzled and repelled by his lover-like advances, thinking of him only as a friend. It is her realisation of the social inappropriateness of this response that sends Stephen off on her unilluminating search for explanations from her father.

The First World War opens up an area of suitably masculine employment for Stephen. She is able to get into uniform and go to the Front as an ambulance-driver. Ironically, the war allows Stephen more opportunities to come into her own and, in the ambulance corps, a world without men, her 'nature' has scope to flourish. Here she finds a suitable partner, Mary Llewelyn, feminine, genuinely loving and an admirer of Stephen's bravery. She is the embodiment of the problem set up by Ellis's theory as to who the true invert's lover could possibly be. She loves Stephen, but is not quite a congenital case herself, being 'all woman', 'perfect woman'. She is womanly and attractive to the masculine Stephen, but then why is she not the lover of a man? The problem is kept in equilibrium in the novel by the social inequality of Mary and Stephen. Stephen is upper-class and Mary an ordinary girl and furthermore, an orphan, with no 'place' in the world.

Their social inequality also serves to make the novel appealing in conventionally romantic terms – someone strong is protecting someone weak from the world, and she is grateful. Stephen provides the displaced Mary with a home after the war and works at her writing to secure Mary's future. Theirs is a very polarised relationship. Stephen is taller, richer, and a stronger character than Mary. The division of labour between them is as stark as in any conventional marriage: Stephen has her writing and Mary, 'the household, the paying of bills, the filing of receipts, the answering of unimportant letters'. Their sexual relationship too is described in very polarised terms, such as, 'Stephen stooped down and kissed her,' or 'she slept in Stephen's masterful arms'. The polarity echoes Ellis's categories of true invert and woman-who-responds-to-true-invert, but fills their relationship out in emotional terms and suggests what might give it stability. It does so of course in terms which feed into the stereotypical images of the lesbian couple, composed of masculine 'butch' and feminine 'femme', far more rigidly than anything Ellis wrote.

Because the homosexual relations described in the novel approximate to those of the heterosexual world, *The Well of Loneliness* is appealing on conventional romantic terms. Even so, the idea that Stephen and Mary's relationship could be a conventional romance is constantly undermined throughout the novel. One source of dissonance is the consistent reference to 'Stephen' as 'she', for example and this dissonance underlines the paradoxical place assigned to lesbianism by theories of congenital inversion. Another source of such dissonance comes through in the way physical sexual relations are dealt with in the novel. Physical sex is clearly implied although not described: it is part of what Hall is arguing to be tolerated by society. But lesbian sex in *The Well* is a recurrent juxtaposition of lesbian passion with images of sterility, unfruitfulness, barrenness, that derive from the comparison with the heterosexual 'norm'. Furthermore, this sterility is seen as somehow inscribed into the body of Stephen the congenital invert – 'this strangely ardent yet sterile body', whose 'barren womb became fruitful – it ached with its fearful and sterile burden'. Sterility is part of the invert's fate and also presented as a misfortune which ought to have a claim on the pity of 'normal' society.

Apart from the spectre of sterility, the passion between Stephen and Mary is shown to be untenable for largely social reasons. What would have counted as a satisfactory *dénouement* in a conventional romantic work here contains the seeds of its own destruction. For Stephen and Mary as a couple, there is social opprobrium from the world at large. Stephen's mother refuses to invite Mary to the house. Their friend, Lady Massey, withdraws an invitation to spend Christmas at her house when the awful truth dawns, having 'her position in the country' to consider. Stephen would have liked to provide a place for Mary in this upper-class milieu and to 'rescue' her from social obscurity, but money and her own social position are insufficient to do this. A rather bitter contrast is drawn with the approval shown to (legitimate) heterosexual alliances: 'Oh, yes, the whole world smiled on Violet and her Alec. "Such a charming young couple", said the world, and at once started to shower them with presents, Apostle teaspoons arrived in their dozens ... '

In fact the only society in which Stephen and Mary can find a niche is the lesbian 'ghetto' which has started to emerge in Paris. Stephen's attitude to this group is extremely ambiguous and contradictory. She is prepared to mix with them because Mary needs friends, but refers to them as a 'miserable army' of inverts, the dregs of society. While thus distancing herself from them, however, Stephen also identifies with them, recognising that, like herself, they have their deviant natures stamped into their physical make-up. Masculine 'symptoms' are remarked upon: 'One might have said quite a womanly woman, unless the trained ear had been rendered suspicious by her voice which had something peculiar about it. It was like a boy's voice on the edge of breaking.'

It is something to be allowed to live as an invert accepted by this group but such ghettoised existence is not enough for Stephen whose vision stretches 'out beyond to the day when happier folk would accept her.' The world of the Paris inverts is a bohemian milieu and Stephen views it from a definite class position in the world at large. The group Stephen and Mary mix with is relatively decent, meeting at teas and 'studio parties'; it is friendly and welcoming to like natures. But the Paris bars – the Ideal, whose 'patron' collects inverts like rare specimens, Le Narcisse, mirrors thickly painted with cupids and kitchen near the toilet, and most of all, Alec's, a drug-dealing haunt – are such as to prove that inverts have been trodden down to become the dregs of humanity. Stephen's upper-class social position vies with a sense of hidden connection with these degraded inverted natures, and she assumes a protective yet superior role towards the 'dregs'. She seems to stand somewhere between them and God, interceding for them: 'She could see their marred and reproachful faces with the haunted, melancholy eyes of the invert – eyes that had looked too long on a world that lacked all pity and understanding: "Stephen, Stephen, speak with your God and ask Him why He has left us forsaken!" ' It is a role conceived of in religious as well as class terms.

In fact, the social context of Stephen's anomalous being and her relations to the rest of the world are described from the beginning of the story. The repercussions of her innate inversion on the rest of her family are depicted from childhood on. There are servants who know her from a child and think or do not think she is just like her father; there is Angela's irate husband, Stephen's censorious mother, and the necessity for a social cover-up from the village of the true state of affairs. But it also perfectly true that this wider social world in which Stephen grows up and with which the lesbian sub-culture is contrasted, is indelibly upper-class.

The particular way in which Stephen grows up 'masculine' is in fact saturated with class. What she grows up to be is a 'perfect gentleman'. From an early age she is instinctively gallant and protective to her mother and by extension to all women; she has a strict sense of honour and speaks of doing 'the decent, clean thing'; she lays on a generous wedding for her servants. The final proof of her moral excellence comes when she gives up the unwitting Mary to Martin, her own old beau, having decided that Mary is too weak and womanly to withstand life without a husband, children and a place in respectable society. These class-bound manifestations of *noblesse oblige* are read back into Stephen's nature just as much as her 'inversion' is. Ellis's suggestion that inverts are rescued by general superiority of character is given a very class-bound interpretation by Hall and one which was felt at the book's trial to make the lesbian character dangerously attractive. The highly moral tone of the book was to count heavily against it – especially as it made an appeal to religion in demanding tolerance. The religious aspect of the book owes nothing to Ellis's theorising. It views Stephen as set apart by God and describes her as 'God's mistake', and 'having the mark of Cain'. The Christian martyr's name, 'Stephen', is actually given at her christening, rather than being a nickname she chooses to adopt.

In the final passage of the novel, which involves a very florid appeal for tolerance and highlights lesbian suffering, it is made clear that Stephen has taken on a religious duty, the task of interceding with society and with God on behalf of all inverts: 'Acknowledge us, oh God, before the whole world. Give us also the right to our existence!' While some of the more serious commentators on the novel deplored the use of religion in such a cause, some of the more cynical were to turn her religious framework against Hall and accuse her of a certain degree of self-martyrdom. But there is no doubt that she used it to add to the poignancy of the suffering of the 'inverts', to intensify the emotional appeal of her novel.

Taken as a whole, *The Well of Loneliness* in some ways sets up a *more* rigid definition of lesbianism than Ellis's *Sexual Inversion* had done. The novel more clearly evokes the stereotyped images of lesbians as 'butch' and 'femme', two complementary halves of a couple polarised between the masculine and the feminine, and these are shown to derive from actual practices in an existing sub-culture. Further, the appeal to moral excellence is made in specifically class terms, feeding into current ideas of lesbianism as an aristocratic aberration. It takes on all Ellis's biologism, and the biographical form of the novel enables Hall to describe a woman's whole life as thoroughly permeated by an innate, unfolding 'inversion' and to set up this sexuality as containing the truth of her being.

On the other hand, the political value of the 'congenital' argument is more overtly deployed by Hall, who clearly argues that inverts are not to be blamed. She tried to depict attractive characters and claim sympathy for them by affective means. Although she stepped into the space Ellis had created and defined for lesbianism, Hall made that space more public. This was to mean that others, feminists, for instance, could engage with and challenge that definition in a more publicly accessible way.

I have suggested that Hall's contribution should be seen as the start of a 'reverse discourse', a process by which a category of lesbianism derived from a medical discourse is firstly adopted and then eventually transformed by those defined by it. This implies a degree of political self-consciousness on the part of lesbians, if they are to speak for themselves as a unified group. It is clear that Hall's intervention can be seen as contributing to the formation of that political self-consciousness: later generations of lesbians were to follow her model of public identification even if they repudiated her particular views. What may be less clear is that her intervention in itself was both an adoption of Ellis's category of 'inversion' and an initial step towards transforming it.

Hall's adopted the category 'congenital inversion' in an unproblematic, straightforward way. But precisely because it rigidly segregated lesbians as a separate type of person, it did have the incidental advantage of conferring an *authoritative* right to speak on those women accepting the label. By separating lesbians into a seemingly quite distinct group, the definition laid the basis for a later political solidarity. Hall claimed the right to speak about inversion on the grounds that she herself was an invert, not an expert. This enabled other women either to imitate her, or to engage in a challenge to what she said, but both on the same level of personal experience *as* 'invert'. They could not have done this with Ellis the medical expert. Taking discussion of inversion beyond the medical textbook enabled

Hall to comment on the basis of her own experience about relationships between individuals and on the conditions in which lesbians were actually able to exist in society. This in itself limited the extent to which Ellis's categorisation of individuals into separate 'types' could be seen as an adequate approach to their problems by inverts themselves. A 'reverse discourse' was thus begun.

Inversion was shown as a problem for society to face and not just a moral dilemma for 'inverted' individuals. The conflicting ways that *The Well of Loneliness* was received by commentators were in fact organised around two dominant discourses: the rearguard moralising discourse of 'sin' or 'sickness' which was now challenged by a new, liberal, discourse on inversion as a 'social problem' backed up by medical opinion. A variant of the 'moralising' commentary was a rather satirical strand, addressing the quality of Hall's book primarily as a work of fiction and criticising it in terms of literary merit, in a way which ostensibly side-stepped her views on lesbianism as such. It was within these competing discourses that a battle over the definition of lesbianism was waged.

Trials of The Well

The progressive nature of the 'congenital' view of lesbianism in the context of 1928 can be gauged by the scandalised reaction of a section of the press to Radclyffe Hall's book and by the way it was subsequently taken to trial and condemned as 'obscene'. James Douglas, editor of the *Sunday Express*, made the first vitriolic attack on the novel on 19 August 1928. In the course of his article he called the book an 'intolerable outrage' and one 'designed to display perverted decadence as a martyrdom inflicted upon these outcasts by a cruel society'. He insisted on using the moralistic term 'perversion' rather than the biologically based and morally neutral 'inversion'. He called lesbianism a 'pestilence' and a 'leprosy', and complained: 'The decadent apostles of the most loathsome vices no longer conceal their degeneracy and their degradation.' Mixed in with the hyperbolic language was a series of rejections of the way the novel defined lesbianism as unavoidable rather than a morally reprehensible choice. Specifically, he claimed that the congenital argument was incompatible with the Christian doctrine of free will: inverts were *choosing* to be damned. He obviously regarded lesbianism as a contagious sickness as well as a sin and saw 'propoganda' like Radclyffe Hall's novel as one of the ways in which perverts sought to spread it to others, especially the young. In a notorious phrase, he wrote that he 'would rather give a healthy boy or a healthy girl a phial of prussic acid than this novel.'

He referred to *The Well* as 'a contamination and corruption of English fiction' and there were several appeals to 'Englishness' in his onslaught. The English patience was being sorely tried by the increasing effrontery of homosexuals flaunting themselves overtly in post-war society; the English public was slow to anger but would be merciless in striking down the armies of evil once roused; France and Germany had already lost the battle, but this Christian society should and would cleanse itself. But it was not for any lewd or lascivious detail that the novel was condemned. Rather it was denounced as 'seductive and insidious' for any delicacy or cleverness it might have, since this would tempt the reader to sympathise with Hall's views. Because of the greater publicity the novel would give to these views, Douglas called for its prosecution under 'the existing law'.

This law was the Obscene Publications Act of 1857 which enabled magistrates to destroy a publication as 'obscene' without taking evidence on its literary merits. The English publisher of *The Well*, Jonathan Cape, fearing prosecution, had written to the Home Secretary following Douglas's attack and offered to withdraw the book. But he then had it secretly printed in Paris. The Director of Public Prosecutions eventually took action against it when imported copies were seized. Since it was the book, and not the author, that was on trial the publisher had to defend it and Hall was not allowed to speak in its defence.

The proceedings were held at Bow Street under Sir Chartres Biron. He refused the defence leave to call literary evidence from a range of luminaries, including Virginia Woolf and E.M. Foster, who were prepared to speak for the book's literary merits. Claiming that art and obscenity were not mutually exclusive, Sir Chartres took the power of deciding what was 'obscene' as belonging entirely to him as Chief Magistrate. The test of obscenity under the law was whether the book was likely to 'deprave or corrupt those whose minds are open to such immoral influences and into whose hands it is likely to fall.' This meant that the book's being a novel counted against it, since it was more likely to fall into the hands of a healthy boy or girl. Whether it would corrupt them if it did was what would make it 'obscene', and so the general stance of the book, its general treatment of its theme, could be enough to condemn it without any 'dirty' words or passages.

This was indeed what happened. The defence's emphasis on the novel as a serious treatment of a medical and social problem did not save it; it was condemned as 'obscene' and remaining copies were destroyed. In his judgement, the Chief Magistrate made it clear that his decision had nothing to do with 'gross or filthy' words in the book, nor was it based on the fact that the book dealt with 'unnatural offences between women'. It was the concept of *lesbianism* itself which was seen as dangerous, because the idea of 'congenital inversion' allowed inverts to be described as attractive personalities and especially because it freed them from moral blame. The magistrate foresaw the effects of allowing *The Well of Loneliness* to define the terms in which lesbianism was discussed.

What was being fought over in the court was not simply the description, but the redefinition of lesbianism. After all, lesbianism had been given literary treatment before, without being the cause of prosecution. Indeed, in the same year, Compton Mackenzie published *Extraordinary Women*, his satire of lesbian mores based on the sub-culture in Capri at the time, and this had not been judged obscene – but then it made no claims to educating public opinion, nor to being a serious book, nor to altering definitions.

When the defendants of *The Well of Loneliness* took the case to the Appeal Court, its Chairman made it even more explicit that the book was on trial for its general concept of lesbianism and its general moral stance. He remarked that, 'It is a book which, if it does not condemn unnatural practices, certainly condones them and suggests that those guilty of them should not receive the consequences they deserve to suffer. Put in a word, the view of the Court is that this is a disgusting book, *when properly read*' (emphasis added). In other words, the book had to be read for its underlying concept of lesbianism and not for any surface particularities in the way that it was written. Without resorting to the excesses of Douglas's language, the court's interpretation of 'obscenity' nevertheless made it clear that the law was to uphold his view of lesbianism and that the 'congenital inversion' view was to be resisted entirely. The obscenity law was geared to maintenance of general moral standards and a concept of lesbianism as an avoidable vice or sin was part of those standards.

The American courts decided differently, however. The New York Society for the Suppression of Vice took out a summons against the U.S. publishers of *The Well*, but the case was dismissed in April 1929 in the New York Court of Special Sessions. While conceding that the subject was 'a delicate social problem', the court decided that there was nothing obscene in the way the book was written. Radclyffe Hall's novel did therefore continue to be available in the United States during the time it was prohibited in Britain. Copies bought abroad were clandestinely circulated here; it was reissued in Paris in 1929 already in a sixth impression. In 1948 it was quietly republished in London without repercussions and in 1968 it appeared in paperback; it has recently been published by the feminist publishing house, Virago.

In 1928 a popular satire on the novel, by artist Beresford Egan and journalist P.B. Stephenson, and entitled *The Sink of Solitude*, denounced the moral crusade against the book. Thanks to it, 'millions of shop, office and mill girls have been led to ask the furtive question: What is Lesbianism?' The authors went on to demand a literary censorship of the Sunday papers whose sensationalism was 'sapping the vigour and the vitality of millions of old ladies every morning'.

This lampoon criticised not only the 'sanctimonious sententiousness' of the moral crusaders but also the 'pathetic post-war lesbians with their "mannish" modes and poses' and what its authors saw as the 'sentimental scientificity' of 'psychopaths' like Havelock Ellis, who ponderously sought to 'explain' them. They remarked on the feebleness of *The Well of Loneliness* both as a work of art and as a moral argument. Putting themselves forward as defenders of aesthetic standards,

Beresford Egan's cartoon for *The Sink of Solitude*

they use this stance to dismiss any serious consideration of lesbianism itself. Stephen's career as 'congenital invert' is swiftly lampooned:

> She kicks, she thrives, she grows to man's estate.
> For trousers love she feels, for knickers hate!

They could thus poke fun at Radclyffe Hall from the posture of a 'defender of English literature' without ever having to engage with the concept of congenital inversion. By defending the glorious Sappho as well as Shakespeare, they could dismiss Hall by contrast as mundane, trivial and trite on the grounds of literary merit alone.

The Sink of Solitude also contained scurrilous, Beardsleyesque drawings unmistakably indicating Hall as the self-martyring 'St Stephen' of the captions. Images of Hall elsewhere, such as in the press, tended to convey an uncompromisingly severe personality. A 'masculine' photograph which had appeared alongside the original onslaught in the *Sunday Express* was frequently reproduced. It showed her with short hair, tie and cigarette. Hall's lover Una Troubridge was often depicted alongside her, either shown as presenting the same rather 'masculine' militant front to the world, or, at other times, in very feminine contrast to her. Some perceived the couple as a strictly polarised one. Vera Brittain reviewed *The Well* as a journalist on *Time and Tide*, and was one of the literary witnesses prepared but not called, to give evidence at the trial. In 1968 she published a book assessing the whole occasion retrospectively and in it she quotes the description of a friend who met Radclyffe Hall in 1928:

> My first impression was of someone very goodlooking, in fact handsome, in a masculine way. She was dressed in a tweedy style, mannishly cut clothes. She had a presence and an air of authority ... Lady Troubridge was the exact opposite – very dainty and feminine ... exquisitely, femininely dressed in rather a 'fluffy' style. My mother used to say that Radclyffe Hall always seemed to be the dominant one in any decision which had to made jointly, regarding their orders for refreshment, cakes to be made and sent, and their Christmas orders for chocolates.

In her own person and in her lesbian relationship, Hall was uncompromising in demanding to be accepted as the archetype of the congenital invert.

Vera Brittain's own review of *The Well of Loneliness* in *Time and Tide* in 1928 had in fact picked up its polarity in the treatment of the lesbian couple and from a feminist point of view had even questioned the view of sex roles as biologically determined. She wrote:

> The book, however, raises and never satisfactorily answers another question – the question as to how far the characteristics of Stephen Gordon are physiological and how far they are psychological ... Miss Hall seems to take for granted that this over-emphasis of sex characteristics is part of the correct education of the normal human being; she therefore makes her 'normal' woman clinging and feminine to exasperation and even describes the attitudes towards love as 'an end in itself' as being a necessary attribute to true womanhood.

This criticism of rigidly defined lesbian roles prefigures the views of later generations of lesbians and feminists and their criticisms of the inflexibility and biological inevitability of the 'congenital inversion' theory of lesbianism. At the time, however, the possibility that the 'congenital' view offered, of seeing lesbianism as a social, and not a moral problem, was not to be lightly dismissed. It argued for social tolerance of an inborn 'condition' on the grounds that it could not be helped; the 'social problem' was that of coping with the consequences of the 'invert's' unfortunate nature and this put the onus on society at large, not just on the individual lesbian. Vera Brittain, despite her feminist criticisms of Hall, was therefore careful not to jettison this perspective of lesbianism as a social problem and hastily added that:

> This is not to deny that the problem described by Miss Hall does exist in a grave and urgent form, and that her presentation of it deserves the serious attention of all students of social questions.

Recent arguments for social acceptance of lesbianism have gone beyond and rejected the idea of 'congenital inversion'. Within the women's and gay movements, the claim to *choice* of sexual partners has replaced claims to biological necessity. While rejecting Hall's precise view of lesbianism as innate sexual nature, however, lesbians have wished to retain a definite lesbian identity, but to have the right to define that lesbian label themselves. Some features of the picture of the 'congenital invert' have thereby explicitly been rejected: innate masculinity, for instance, and also the idea that lesbians must be sterile. Lesbians in recent years have claimed the right to be mothers – a contradiction in terms for the 'congenital invert'.

At the time, 'congenital inversion' seemed to be a biological truth which had been 'discovered'. Today, when we have largely rejected this 'truth' and questioned its progressive potential, we can see the category of 'invert' rather as a social construction, a work of definition. Retrospectively, we can see a process beginning with the definition of lesbianism in medical-scientific theory and reaching a point where lesbians have politically articulated a demand to define themselves. Radclyffe Hall has a significant place in that process and her fiction helped to challenge the prevalent view of lesbianism as a reprehensible vice and facilitated its translation from the realm of 'sin' to that of 'social problem'. *The Well of Loneliness* also remained an important definer of lesbian identity for many years. The prosecution of the novel promoted it as a major source of how to 'be' a lesbian in real life. And focusing attention on its author, the book's real-life heroine, the trial unwittingly took the question of lesbianism outside the category of 'fiction'.

Bibliography

Brittain, Vera, *Radclyffe Hall: a case of obscenity?*, Femina Books, London, 1968.
Dyer, Richard,'Getting over the Rainbow', in *Silver Linings*, Lawrence and Wishart, London 1981.
Egan, Beresford, *The Sink of Solitude*, Hermes Press, London, 1928.
Ellis, Henry Havelock, *Sexual Inversion*, Wilson and Macmillan, London, 1897. *Studies in the Psychology of Sex*, Philadelphia, 1905 – 1910; Random House, New York 1936.
Foucault, Michel, *The History of Sexuality*, Allen Lane, London, 1979.
Hall, Marguerite Radclyffe, *The Well of Loneliness*, Jonathan Cape, London

1928; Blue Ribbon Books, New York 1928 Covici-Friede Inc; New York 1928, Pegasus Press Paris, 1928; reprinted 1929: Falcon Press London, 1948: Permabooks, New York, 1960; Transworld Publishers, London (Corgi), 1968; Virago Press, London, 1981.

Mackenzie, Compton, *Extraordinary Women*, London 1928.

Weeks, Jeffrey, *Coming Out*, Quartet, London, 1977.

Feminism and the Definition of Cultural Politics

Michèle Barrett

Cultural politics are crucially important to feminism because they involve struggles over *meaning*. The contemporary Women's Liberation Movement has, by and large, rejected the possibility that our oppression is caused by either naturally given sex differences or economic factors alone. We have asserted the importance of consciousness, ideology, imagery and symbolism for our battles. Definitions of femininity and masculinity, as well as the social meaning of family life and the sexual division of labour, are constructed on this ground. Feminism has politicized everyday life – culture in the anthropological sense of the lived practices of a society – to an unparalleled degree. Feminism has also politicized the various forms of artistic and imaginative expression that are more popularly known as culture, reassessing and transforming film, literature, art, the theatre and so on.

Immediately we begin to think about this it becomes difficult to say exactly what is meant by cultural politics. If I spray-paint a sexist advertisement this is quite clearly cultural politics. But if I do it so imaginatively that a feminist photographer captures it for the walls of an alternative art gallery, has my illegal graffiti then become feminist art? The distinction between art and culture is a vexed one, but there are political (as well as academic) reasons for thinking it through further.

Raymond Williams, who recently published a book entitled *Culture* (Williams, 1981), sensibly refuses to give a snap definition of the term. Instead he outlines the historical meanings of the concept and discusses more recent influences on his own use of it. To the anthropological and popular uses that I have already mentioned he adds the current interest in 'signification' – systems of signs, cutting across the conventional division between art and popular culture, through which meaning is constructed, represented, consumed and reproduced.* But if culture is difficult to define, art is certainly impossible. In the absence of any convincing account of what is intrinsically 'aesthetic', art can only be that which is defined as art in a particular society at a particular time. Indeed the category of 'art' is not a universal one.

I raise these problems at the outset since the purpose of this paper is to question what we mean by art and culture in the context of current feminist practice. Is a work of art a battleground for ideological struggle in the same way as a sexist poster? Or are there qualities to art that render a directly political approach less relevant? To engage in cultural politics is to take a stance on these questions and it is here that I want to start.

I. When Is Art Feminist Art?

Bearing these problems in mind I want to look first at how we could describe something such as a film or a painting as 'sexist' or 'feminist'. Recent films such as *Girlfriends*, or *An Unmarried Woman*, or *Coma*, all depict women as less passive and dependent than they were in previous commercial films. This leads us to ask in what sense they might be called 'feminist' films. We notice that the sanctified orthodoxy of the soap opera

---

* Williams summarizes the present co-ordinates of the term 'culture' as follows: 'Thus there is some practical convergence between (i) the anthropological and sociological senses of culture as a distinct "whole way of life", within which, now, a distinctive "signifying system" is seen not only as essential but as essentially involved in *all* forms of social activity, and (ii) the more specialized if also more common sense of culture as "artistic and intellectual activities", though these, because of the emphasis on a general signifying system, are now much more broadly defined, to include not only the traditional arts and forms of intellectual production but also all the "signifying practices" – from language through the arts and philosophy to journalism, fashion and advertising – which now constitute this complex and necessarily extended field.'

is being invaded by the introduction of dangerous topics like abortion or the double standard of sexual morality, and we wonder whether a feminist has actually managed to get a job on *Crossroads* or *The Archers*. *Spare Rib*, by far the most widely read feminist magazine in this country, devotes a lot of space to reviews of the media and the arts and many of them turn on the question of *how feminist* are the particular books or shows being reviewed. This is a fairly clear-cut issue when we think of an appallingly degrading advertisement or a polemical new novel by a well-known feminist, but the grey area between them is much more difficult to assess. And yet this grey area covers an enormous amount of ground. Let us take just two examples.

A controversy has arisen on the question of pornography. Many feminists will argue that pornography, certainly as produced in contemporary Britain, is not merely sexist but an expression of male violence against women which must be confronted and eradicated. The images of pornography are seen as directly exploitative of, and degrading to, women and they are linked to rape and other forms of male violence. The 'Reclaim the Night' movement highlights this connection in its political campaign to make the streets safe for women by siting its demonstrations in areas like Soho where sex-shops and sex-cinemas abound. Many feminists nonetheless feel ambivalent or opposed to blanket censorship. When, they ask, is erotica pornography and vice-versa? To some degree the problem lies in the fact that an image itself is not necessarily either pornography *or* erotica – it becomes so when viewed as such. Some feminist bookshops recognize this by roping off a 'women only' section of lesbian erotica: to us it's a legitimate artistic celebration of female sexuality but for voyeuristic men it would be pornography.

The women's group at my college put on a play by a feminist theatre group in which a rape scene was depicted and it was clear that the meaning of the scene was very different for the feminists at the front and the men from the rugby club who rushed in from the bar (laughing) when they heard what was going on. So the image itself, or the play or whatever, might not necessarily be intrinsically sexist or feminist, it may depend on who is reading or receiving it and how they do so. The image itself may often be ambiguous, at least partially open to the different meanings we choose to construct upon it.

This ambiguity is present in all art forms, not only in the visual arts where it is perhaps most widely recognized. My second example comes from literature. Feminist literary critics have drawn attention to the impassioned rebellion against male definitions of women's lot which have from time to time erupted in the work of even the most classical of female novelists.

Charlotte Brontë is a case in point. Her novels contain many passages of overt feminist polemic and display a profound scepticism about the ideology of romantic love as it affects women. Let us look at one passage which can easily be read as a feminist protest. In her novel *Shirley* Brontë describes the feelings of Caroline Helstone for the man she loves. One evening he is sufficiently warm to her for her to feel that he returns her love but he, in fact, must be wary of falling for a woman as poor as Caroline and when she meets him the next day he is cold and withdrawn towards her. Caroline is bitterly disappointed and Charlotte Brontë writes:

> A lover masculine so disappointed can speak and urge explanation; a lover feminine can say nothing; if she did, the result would be shame and anguish, inward remorse for self-treachery. Nature would brand such demonstration as a rebellion against her instincts, and would vindictively repay it afterwards by the thunderbolt of self-contempt smiting suddenly in secret. Take the matter as you find it; ask no questions; utter no remonstrances: it is your best wisdom. You expected bread and you have got a stone; break your teeth on it, and don't shriek because the nerves are martyrised: do not doubt that your mental stomach – if you have such a thing – is strong as an ostrich's: the stone will digest. You held out your hand for an egg, and fate put into it a scorpion. Show no consternation: close your fingers firmly upon the gift; let it sting through your palm. Never mind: after your hand and arm have swelled and quivered long with torture, the squeezed scorpion will die, and you will have learned the great lesson how to endure without a sob. For the whole remnant of your life, if you survive the test – some, it is said, die under it – you will be stronger, wiser, less sensitive. This you are not aware of, perhaps, at the time, and so cannot borrow courage of that hope. Nature, however, as has been intimated, is an excellent friend in such cases; sealing the lips interdicting utterance, commanding a placid dissimulation: a dissimulation often wearing an easy and gay mien at first, settling

down to sorrow and paleness in time, then passing away, and leaving a convenient stoicism, not the less fortifying because it is half-bitter (Brontë, 1965: 81-82).

It would not be surprising if a contemporary feminist 'reading' of this passage stressed the progressiveness of this angry yet perceptive outburst. The stone on which we must break our teeth and the scorpion we must suffer to crush are extreme and uncompromising images which resonate with our own passionate anger. Yet we should not be led into projecting too much onto passages such as this one. It is, on closer reading, an ambivalent outburst. How seriously do we take Brontë's reference to 'nature' as the source of our suffering? It is all too easy to invoke the convenient literary critical notion of 'irony' and credit Brontë with satirizing the assumption that women's inferior situation is naturally given. But are we justified in doing so when even the passage quoted, let alone the overall tenor of her novels, expresses a clear belief in resignation, in stoicism, as the characterful resolution of such anguish?

The passage quoted is ambivalent and contradictory. A novel by Charlotte Brontë can be read neither as a feminist polemic nor as an unconscious expression of attitudes to femininity current in her lifetime. One way in which literary critics have tried to throw light on the supposed intended meaning of the text is by examining the life and beliefs of the author. But this is not necessarily of much use to us. We know, for instance, that Charlotte Brontë suffered from and railed against the constraints imposed upon women of her class at that period; we also know that at the end of her life she married and settled down with a man she was not in love with. Facts such as these may or may not throw much light on the question of 'how feminist' the novels are. I suspect they do not. Further, and this is a serious problem, I suspect that if we are honest about it we might admit that our reading of such texts is profoundly influenced by our knowledge of the sex of the author: in *Shirley*, when Charlotte Brontë refers to 'nature' we credit her with an ironic exposure of the irrationality of socially constructed ideologies, but if a man had written the same passage we could be accusing him of biologism. This can be a dangerous route to an interpretation of fiction – not least in that it ignores the fact that the work in question is one of *fiction* – a point I shall come back to later.

For the moment I want simply to note two points. First, that the 'sexism' or 'feminism' of particular works of art or images is not self-evident, or in any unambiguous way intrinsic to that work, but depends upon how we read it. Second, that knowledge of the sex of the author cannot be a reliable guide to the meaning of the text – it cannot tell us what the intentions of the author might have been and in any case these do not necessarily give us the meaning of the text as different readers experience it. I am not disputing that an image or text carries with it a dominant, or preferred, reading and that the relationship between the consumer and the work is one in which meaning is constructed within a particular range of options. But I want to suggest that this given range of meaning may serve to identify the issues at stake rather than determine an interpretation of them. The text may ensure that we read it in terms of sexual politics, for instance, but it cannot legislate against the reader drawing inferences that are the reverse of those offered by the text.

II. When Is Women's Art Feminist Art?

This leads to a second problem. This is the question asked by Rosalind Coward in her article 'Are Women's Novels Feminist Novels?' (Coward, 1980). Although Coward's piece is directed towards one particular review article on feminist fiction, her argument is in fact a generalized critique of a major (if not the main) tendency in feminist literary criticism. She argues that feminists have emphasized the unity and continuity of women's creative work and have tended to confuse feminist art with, simply, women's art. Coward rejects this conflation of the two, and she suggests that the current popularity of 'women's fiction' is not necessarily feminist at all. Feminism, she argues, is an alignment of political interests and not a shared female experience; hence a tradition of women's art is of no particular importance.

This goes right to the nub of a number of controversial questions about feminism and culture. Is the recovery of women's artistic work of the past an integral part of our developing feminist project, or merely a sentimental resuscitation of marginalia better left in the obscurity to which establishment criticism has consigned it? What do we gain by elevating traditional crafts such as embroidery and knitting to the status of art objects and hanging them in galleries? What is the meaning of an art exhibition where the objects displayed are kitchen utensils or the careful record of a child's upbringing? How should we react to art that claims to be based on a 'female language' or on an artistic rendering of the female body and genitalia? In what sense might these various imaginative comments on women's experience be seen as 'feminist' art? Is a work of art feminist because the artist says it is, or the collective who produced it announce their feminist principles of work?

These questions were crystallized for me in a thought-provoking way by Judy Chicago's exhibition *The Dinner Party*, and although this has not yet been shown in Britain I want to use it to illustrate some points. The leaflet accompanying the show states that ' ... the goal of *The Dinner Party* is to ensure that women's achievements become a permanent part of our culture', and the scale of the exhibition matches this monumental aspiration.

The central conception is a triangular dining-table, along the sides of which are placed symbolic representations of thirty-nine women: pre-Christian goddesses; historical figures such as Sappho and Boadaceia; women like the suffragist Susan B. Anthony and the artist Georgia O'Keefe. (This dining-table echoes the 'last supper' so significant to our male-dominated Christian culture.) Each of the figures at the table has a place setting of a runner, cutlery, goblet and plate, whose different designs evoke her particular character. From these thirty-nine women the names of 999 less resoundingly famous, but still reasonably well-known, women radiate in inscriptions on the 'heritage floor'. Surrounding this central focus of the exhibition are banners designed for the entrance, documentation of the five year's work by Judy Chicago and her team of helpers, an exhibition of china-painting, and a display of congratulatory telegrams from feminist artists all over the world.

The size of the exhibition – completely devoted to women's achievements – is, literally, spectacular. When I saw it an entire floor of the San Francisco Museum of Modern Art had been given over to it. The dining-table itself totals nearly 150 feet in length, each woman's place setting using about three and a half feet of space. The combination of this impressive scale and the lavish, beautiful, solid, ceramics and embroidery made the experience of being there an obviously moving one for many women. Never before, it seemed, had women taken over the cultural arena in such a flamboyant and confident way. The atmosphere, too, was wonderful – bringing back all the most positive and sisterly dimensions of a large women's liberation conference since there were so many feminists there.

The experience of being there was for me a striking one and I warmed immediately to the project. It conveyed a real sense of women's achievements and perhaps we too frequently refuse to take pride in them. The feeling of straightforward gender-congratulation was a new and welcome one. Yet in other respects the exhibition was extremely disturbing.

First, it was clear from the documentation that Judy Chicago had not only conceived the project but had directed the work of her many assistants with a positively dictatorial zeal. The principles of collective work vaunted here were not so much the ones I might recognize as feminist but an attempt to recreate the 'school' or studio of an 'Artistic Genius' like Michaelangelo. Although hundreds of people gave much time and work to the project it is Judy Chicago personally who has, apparently not unwillingly, made an international reputation from it.

Second, we have to question whether it is necessarily progress to retrieve embroidery and china-painting from the inglorious role of women's drudgery (or at best 'craft') and re-allocate them to the realm of 'high art'. This is undoubtedly the aim of the show, and it is one that is fraught with problems What has happened to previous radical artists who attempted to challenge prevailing definitions of the 'appropriate' contents of art galleries? This is not a reactionary question, for the answer is that by and large their iconoclasm has been effectively dampened by a versatile establishment and so their challenge to the institution has been converted into artistic novelty. To sail into the establishment without seeing this as a problem is to beg the question of what 'art' is and how it differs from other forms of work. It is not enough simply to get what women do

The Dinner Party, 1979, Judy Chicago (*above*)

Following:

The Dinner Party detail: Virginia Woolf place-setting

Spray-painted advertisement, London 1979, by Jill Posener

Spray-painted advertisement, London 1981, by Jill Posener

If it were a lady, it would pinch its bottom

If it were a lady, it would get its bottom pinched.

If this lady was a car she'd run you down.

FIAT

The beautiful 127 Palio.

TO VOLVO, A SON. 4,397 POUNDS.

recognized as 'art'.

Third, I found the uncritical exercise of ranking 'great women' rather disturbing. There is something rather crude in deeming (to take some British examples of the figures used) the composer Ethel Smythe and the writer Virginia Woolf as worthy of individual places at the dining-table, while Jane Austen and Dorothy Wordsworth merit only an inscription on the floor. The heroines of feminism are here graded, ranked according to a set of criteria that are highly subjective. (On what grounds was it decided that Eleanor of Acquitaine made a greater contribution to feminism than the Virgin Mary? Is there not something bizarre in ranking Emily Dickinson with the Primordial Goddess?) The list of names in the catalogue is studded with epithets like 'pioneer', 'prizewinning', 'cultural leader' and 'eminent intellectual' – all of them terms of evaluation which we have developed a critical stance towards. The search for heroines and role models, for the great women of history, is one which raises a number of difficulties.

Finally, there are the problems surrounding how these women are represented in the exhibition. It is, perhaps, unsurprising and even appropriate that mythological goddesses are symbolized through renderings of clitoral and vaginal imagery. We have little to know them by. But for other women, of whose lives and beliefs we know far more (since they are historical rather than mythological figures), the inevitable vaginal imagery is less appropriate. Less appropriate! I was in fact horrified to see a 'Virginia Woolf' whose image to me represented a reading of her life and work which contradicted all she had ever stood for. There she sits: a genital sculpture in deep relief (about four inches high) resting on a runner of pale lemon gauze with the odd blue wave embroidered on it. Gone is Woolf's theory of androgyny and love of gender ambiguity; gone the polemical public voice; gone the complex symbolic abstractions of her writing. I found this exclusive emphasis on genitalia, and the sentimentality of the trappings, a complete betrayal – as was the 'Emily Dickinson' whose vagina is trimmed with a white lace effect over the palest pink. Very few of our celebrated sisters manage to escape this dreadful posthumous fate. Ethel Smythe appears here as a rather fine grand piano on a background of grey pin-stripe, but this, one fears, is attributable to Chicago's perceptions of her as a dyke. It is in fact typical of Chicago's somewhat biologistic approach to feminism that various of the protagonists are credited for creating a 'female form' of art or literature – in itself a controversial achievement since the possible existence of 'female' forms of art has yet to be established. The notion that some forms of art are intrinsically female (or male) is a dubious one.

All these reservations about *The Dinner Party* have a bearing on the problem of what can be said to be feminist art. This particular case is of interest in that Chicago's claims for the exhibition – that it serves her project of securing artistic recognition for women's achievements – crystallize one specific approach to feminist cultural politics. Her argument that women's art is systematically excluded from the artistic establishment is demonstrated by the fact that after an immensely popular American tour the show went into storage rather than on to Europe.

But problems still remain in (i) the difficulty of arriving at a consensus among feminists as to what constitutes 'feminist' art and (ii) the fact that the use of women's lives, histories and experience does not necessarily ensure the coherent, feminist, reading of Chicago's work that the artist appears to desire. In this sense the case of *The Dinner Party* does seem to me to illustrate the truth of Rosalind Coward's warning that women's art is not necessarily feminist art. Feminist art is not the same as any art which emphasizes women's experience.

We cannot, however, completely separate feminist art from women's experience and hence I would not go so far as Rosalind Coward when she writes:

> Feminism can never be the product of the identity of women's experiences and interests – there is no such unity. Feminism must always be the alignment of women in a political movement with particular political aims and objectives. It is a grouping unified by its *political interests*, not by its common experiences (Coward, 1980:63).

Whatever the problems of basing feminism on the experience shared by women, far greater problems arise in attempting completely to divorce feminism (as a political project) from women's experience. This leads to the position that women's shared experience of oppression plays no significant part in the construction of a feminist cultural politics, which in turn must lead to the conclusion that feminist art could equally well be developed by (for instance) a man. Although an emphasis on women's experience, or the fact of female authorship, or indeed a concern with the female body, is not enough to make a work of art feminist I do not see how feminism can ever take women to be a dispensable category. So although I agree that an emphasis on women is not a sufficient condition to make cultural production feminist it must at least be a *necessary* condition. Put another way, feminist art could be seen as a category *within* a tradition of women's art but I fail to see how it could be generated outside it. It may be that in general women's art is only indirectly useful or inspiring to feminism, but it is not possible to conceive of a feminist art that could be detached from a shared experience of oppression.

III. When is Culture 'Art'?

The third issue I want to take up is the rather thorny one of what we mean by 'art'. This is very difficult to approach in a direct way, since our ideas about art are profoundly influenced by, and entangled with, a particular historical conception of art which affects feminist as well as other types of thinking.

Elaine Showalter has pointed out that feminist criticism has tended to take two clearly identifiable paths (Showalter, 1979). She calls the first 'feminist critique'. This is the study of woman as reader, and it concentrates on woman as a reader of male literature, emphasizing the sexist assumptions of that body of art. The second she calls 'gynocritics', the study of woman as writer in which we can explore the development of a female literary tradition. If this is an accurate account, which it probably is, then it reflects rather badly on feminist criticism. For it represents a way of looking at literature which completely separates the activity of reading (consumption) from that of writing (production). It assumes that art is produced by specialized individuals ('artists') and passively consumed by everyone else. This assumption is deeply engrained in our

culture. Our entire education system is based on the
assumption (to simplify a little) that small children enjoy
splashing about with paint, banging drums and writing stories,
but that by the time we reach the end of secondary school we
will have naturally separated into the uncreative majority and
the few who go on to study or practise 'art'. For most adults the
world of art is one which other people make for us – for our
edification, enjoyment or entertainment. It comes as a shock to
us to realize that in other cultures, and in our own in the past,
art was not thought to be the province of particular individuals
but was distributed more evenly across all social activity.

Without going into the question of how and why this specific
social role of 'the artist' came about, it is clear that we have
inherited a conception of art as something removed from other
forms of social activity. Art is seen as the antithesis of work. It is
mythologized as an oasis of creativity in the desert of alienated
mass-production capitalism. It is idealized as the inspired
product of a few gifted and privileged people, constructed on
we know not what principles and existing in a kind of other-
worldly limbo. It is credited with the ability to transcend the
'real world', lifting us into an arena of higher experience.
Confronted with a 'masterpiece' we are to wonder, dumbly, at
the unimaginable talent that went into making it. The viewer
takes a humble distance from the artist.

To challenge these myths is to raise some interesting
questions. If we reject the view that art is necessarily different
from work we find ourselves considering afresh the ways in
which artistic production may be akin to other forms of social
production.

Janet Wolff, in *The Social Production of Art* (Wolff, 1981),
argues that the work involved in producing an artistic or
imaginative work is not essentially different from other forms of
work. Marx's well-known remark on the difference between the
worst of architects and the best of bees (that the former raises
the structure in the imagination before starting to
build) stresses the fact that human labour is based on the
creative act of planning. It is only the degradation of work
under capitalist relations of production, including the degree to
which workers have been stripped of mental control over their
labour, that makes us perceive such a huge gulf between work

and what we call 'creative' work.

Marxists working in the field of aesthetics have tried to develop an analysis of artistic production and, to a lesser extent, of distribution and consumption of art. One central question, however, tends to remain evaded or unsatisfactorily dealt with. This is the question of aesthetic value. I want to raise it again here because it has not yet been resolved in feminist thinking about art and we tend to operate with varying sets of assumptions on this question.

The problem posed by 'aesthetic value' is a very simple one: are some works of art 'better' than others and, if it is possible to say that they are, then how do we justify our judgements? Literary and art critics have been renowned for the ease, if not arrogance, with which they have presumed definitively to rank works of art or individual artists in levels of greatness. In a more everyday sense people will often confidently say that something is 'good', not necessarily linking this to whether they 'liked' the work in question or not. A high level of confidence in such judgements seems to have been common until well into this century, when this exercise came to be challenged seriously. The challengers have tended to criticize the assumption that 'aesthetic value' exists as a universal category, manifested as an intrinsic property of certain works of art, and have pointed to the political character of such judgements – they are biased towards the artistic production of dominant social groups. To recognize this is inevitably to cast suspicion on the objectivity and universality of the criteria used to rank art.

A number of possible arguments flow from this recognition.

1) The first would be to say that because judgements of aesthetic value have always been not merely culturally-bound but the expression of dominant groups within particular cultures we can therefore have no confidence in them at all. In a radical rejection of the claim that aesthetic value can be assessed objectively we can then arrive at the view that any art is as good as any other. The poem you scribble on the back of an envelope is every bit as good as the sonnet by D.H.Lawrence that F.R. Leavis admires.

2) A second response would be to argue that aesthetic value does exist as an objective category, and that our task is to remove political prejudice from its measurement. Our role is to

insist on the value of the work usually ignored or rejected by the critical establishment. Where they tend to value the work of the white, male bourgeoisie we must insist on the value of working class culture, or women's art, or black art. According to this view our task would be to struggle with the arbiters of aesthetic value and force them to assent to a high value being placed on excellent instances of minority culture. When the league-table of great artists is drawn up we want our candidates up there at the top.

3) A third possibility is to resolve the apparent conflict between aesthetic value and political value by attempting to construct an explicit relationship between the two – in essence, to argue that far from being divorced from political significance, aesthetic value should in fact be attributed on the basis of political progressiveness. Using this view rather loosely we could argue that feminism at present can and should regard art that is firmly located in women's experience and that points to a less oppressive future as of great value – as 'good' in a particular historical and political context.

None of these views is ultimately satisfactory though, and I think this is because they all evade the problem of how we can specify what really constitutes aesthetic value. The first view tends towards complete relativism – aesthetic value is merely judged according to political prejudice and is not a meaningful category – and leaves us with total inability to distinguish between a random scrawl and a finely-wrought painting that has moved generations of people. The second view is somewhat uncritical of existing criteria used for judging aesthetic value and in practice tends to lead towards unconvincing conclusions. Is it really only because of male dominance in art history that we think Rembrandt a 'better' painter than Angelica Kauffman, or because of patriarchal criticism that we find Stendhal a 'better' novelist than Marie Corelli? The third view evades the problem altogether, simply abandoning any notion of value which is independent of the political significance of the work at the time it was produced.

It might be possible to side-step some of these difficulties by asking a rather provocative question. Is it feasible to rehabilitate a category of objectively judged aesthetic value? The answer to this question could in fact be yes, and in exploring this we might be able to consider afresh two problems raised by contemporary 'radical' approaches to art. These two problems are *imagination* and *skill*. Neglect of both of these, in feminist as in Marxist aesthetics, has led to some of the difficulties and confusions I have already touched on. So I want to put forward the proposition that skill and imagination have played a larger part in the construction of art than many radical critics have chosen to think.

We can think about the question of skill by referring back to the idea that artistic production is not essentially unlike other forms of social production. Now, although we know that social definitions of skill are the product of struggle (in that particular groups of workers have succeeded in achieving definition of their work as skilled while other groups doing similar work have lacked the bargaining power to do this), it cannot be denied that there is an objective element to skill. We can all recognize that a television engineer, a typesetter, a midwife, have skills that have been learnt. Similarly we grant that acting, stage design, pottery or tapestry are skilled crafts. The distinctions between 'work', 'craft' and 'art' are difficult to maintain when we consider the question of skill. We have little hesitation in attributing and estimating skill in work such as decorating, and the concept of craft is popularly identified with training and skill. Yet a curious indulgence sets in when we come to consider art – we are reluctant to see it in terms of the skills by which it was produced, partly no doubt because we are so badly-educated in art that often we cannot even assess the skills involved. We cannot see how a particular effect was achieved. Yet skill plays a central role in artistic production, and the most brilliantly imaginative idea will be frustrated if we lack the skill to execute and express it. There are many problems attached to assessing artistic skill, but we gain nothing by avoiding them and pretending that skill is not a crucial element in the production of art.

On the face of it there seems to be no need to point to imagination as a defining characteristic of art, since the popular view of art is to perceive it exclusively in these terms. Radical criticism has, however, tended to reject this view to the point of virtually denying the imaginative character of art. The everyday meaning of fiction (the antithesis to fact) is forgotten by a radical aesthetics that has seen fiction as a descriptive category, like painting or sculpture. All too often fiction is treated solely in terms of the social reading we can make of it, the points where we can pin it down by its social or psychic determinants. This approach to fiction rests on a more or less crude application of sociological content analysis. In its more vulgar form it looks for the reflection in fiction of social fact, historical reality; in its more sophisticated form it sees fiction as a site in which various possible extra-textual elements can be located and dissected out. Yet in all this we often forget that fiction has a very oblique relation to the social reality to which we are trying to link it. This is precisely because fiction is an imaginative construction and is hence not a reliable indicator of social reality. We can never know exactly what relation a particular fictional work bears to the historical context of its production. Obviously to some extent, as Terry Eagleton points out, every work ' ... encodes within itself its own ideology of how, by whom and for whom it was produced' (Eagleton, 1976:48); but this should not lead us to believe that the only way in which we can relate to the work is by trying to decode it. Such decoding exercises may be very useful, but cannot ultimately provide all that we need to know about the work.

There is, then, something to be gained from rehabilitating what is currently thought of as a rather reactionary view of art. Within specific aesthetic forms and conventions we may be able to identify different levels of skill as well as the expression of particular fictional, or imaginative, constructions of reality. To point to this is not to slide into the individualistic romanticism of traditional bourgeois theories of art; it is merely to indicate the extent to which radical criticism has abandoned this dimension of art altogether.

To assert the possibility of critical and imaginative consciousness brings certain advantages to our thinking about art. It may, for instance, enable us not to separate so rigidly and disastrously the aspects of artistic production and consumption. For if we can identify levels of aesthetic skill in the construction of works of art, and the expression of critical and fictional representation of the world, it becomes clear that the reading of the work will inevitably depend upon the corresponding consciousness and knowledge of the audience.

The more we understand about the principles, and skills required, for the construction of particular works the more completely we shall be able to receive them. The more we share, or identify with, a particular consciousness of the world the more we shall enter into a fictional rendering of that consciousness. Hence the rehabilitation of a specifically aesthetic level of meaning may enable us to see why works of art cannot be understood either as *intrinsically* feminist (or anything else), or as *necessarily* carrying a meaning determined by the authors' intentions. The meaning they have is constructed in our consumption of them and it becomes impossible to separate the production of the work from its consumption.

What are the implications of this for feminist cultural politics? First, a priority would be to try and break down the idealization of the 'artist', which occurs as frequently in feminist culture as elsewhere. We need to reject the notion that women's liberation needs feminist artists to inspire us for more mundane struggles and move towards a greater acknowledgement of the reciprocal character of art in the social construction of political meaning. We need to work towards the creation of a cultural milieu in which feminist vision is creatively consumed as well as imaginatively produced. In this context an emphasis on aesthetic skills is in fact *democratizing* rather than elitist – for skills may be acquired, whereas the notion of an artistic 'genius' forbids the aspirations of anyone outside the small and specialized group. Differences in individual aptitude do not affect this generalization. Secondly, it suggests that we need to rethink our attitude towards the type of interventions currently being made in cultural politics. Two particular aspects of this will be taken up now, and they are the role of avant-gardism in feminist art, and the question of pleasure and the moralism surrounding it.

IV. Should Cultural Politics be Pleasurable?

The problem of avant-gardism can be put quite simply: given that there is a limited amount of energy available, should feminists be working at the frontiers developing new forms of expression or attempting to influence the mass media and reach a wider audience? The case for a feminist avant-garde appears to me to rest on two propositions. The first is that feminism will not only inform what is said, but will inform *how* it is said and therefore new forms of expression must be created. In its strongest form this argument will tend to suggest that existing art forms are by nature male, or patriarchal, and that a women's language and style must be developed. The second proposition is that existing art forms tend to be supportive of the status quo and that there is something intrinsically radical about breaking with them. This view tends to hark back to the debates between the modernists and realists earlier this century, when modernists claimed that their insistent refusal to meet the reader's expectations, their intransigent denial of the anticipated structure and resolution of 'the story', was of itself revolutionary.

There are a number of limitations to both of these positions. For while it is true that there is a difference in what is represented in the cultural production of men and women, and the representation of gender in works of art tends in itself to be gendered by the author, it does not necessarily follow that the particular art forms or languages are intrinsically gendered. On the second point the arguments are more complex. The question as to whether rupturing the artistic status quo is necessarily progressive or revolutionary is a difficult one. This difficulty lies partly in the point made earlier on the active reception of the audience in setting cultural meaning. An innovatory piece of work may be experienced as such, or as startling, shocking, disturbing, if the audience is sufficiently familiar with the conventions it seeks to challenge and subvert. But is it necessarily significant in this respect when it is not perceived as such? This may depend upon our knowledge of the medium and the subtlety or otherwise of our response. I am aware, for example, that, while I can see for myself a departure from tradition in a contemporary novel, I have to be told by others that such and such a camera angle or style of shot constitutes a rejection of bourgeois practice in film-making. So the innovativeness depends at least to some degree on a relationship to knowledge of an earlier practice.

In so far as the claims to progressiveness of the avant-garde rest on arguments similar to those put forward by the modernists, they invite a similar question: avant-garde (modernist) in relation to what? These are necessarily relative terms and we relate to the new on the basis of our experience of the old. I am not trying to suggest that experimental work is not important, merely arguing that, as with all forms of artistic production, it must be defined and limited by the audience receiving it at any particular time. In this sense there is not any significant difference between the processes involved in challenging the expectations of a minority audience of contemporary experimental film or music, and challenging the expectations of a very large television audience.

It follows from all this that a strong distinction between 'art' (with an experimental avant-garde) and 'the mass media' (with critical infiltration) is not altogether viable. In both cases the role of a critical political intervention is to challenge accepted conventions and representations and to offer a different consciousness of the world and how it might be changed. Given that there is this similarity, we perhaps pay insufficient attention to the political gains that might be made by a larger-scale challenge to the media. From the point of view of political strategy it could be profitable to question the emphasis on some of the more purist elements of feminist thinking on aesthetics. No doubt it is true that within radical cultural practice it is possible to pose more fundamental questions and proffer more profound transformations than within the media, but a small popular change is *relatively* just as significant as a large minority change. There may be at least as much potential for change in a tv soap opera as in agit-prop theatre. One reason why this has been somewhat neglected (and here I do want to be critical of a tendency within the avant-garde), is the prevalence of moralism. The mass media is often seen as inescapably locked in an illusory construction of pleasure – pleasure in a created complacency. Television and the popular cinema are seen as pandering to a reprehensible desire on the part of the audience for romance, violence, identification, a good yarn, an illusion of stability and closure. The denial of pleasure, the refusal to resolve ambiguity and conflict into consensus and conservatism, is a hallmark of the avant-garde. It has brought with it a moralistic purism, which I now want to discuss.

The question of pleasure is a particularly provoking one. In cultural politics it frequently surfaces as an irritation: *why* do people enjoy things that are politically bad for them? Among feminists the problem is often acute. What is the nature of the illicit pleasure 'she' takes in a happy ending? Why do we still take pleasure in fashion magazines, or the dashing exploits of ' male heroes, or lyrical love songs, or blatant sentimentality? What meaning can we attach to these pleasures and our ambivalence about them?

The response of feminist critics and aestheticians has often been tinged with, not to say predicated upon, a form of moralism. No feminist could enjoy a book by Barbara Cartland or Norman Mailer and if you do then so much the worse for your feminism. Is your pleasure in Garbo or Fonda politically correct? Does it rest on the extent to which, for their time, they express a feminist point of view? Or something else not so worthy? Can you legitimate your ambivalent views on camp?

All this stems from a desire to reject a sexist culture and develop a feminist alternative. In the long run this moralism suffers from the limitations of all lifestyle politics. In the first place it requires such an investment of energy that the construction of an alternative within existing culture can sap the energy available for strategies directed at more fundamental changes. In the second place it can divert us from examining our own ambivalence and from understanding more about our pleasure. To refuse such an examination is utopian. Without sinking into total complacency we can try to get to grips with some aspects of pleasure. We have not only our own consciousness to consider. How can we widen the purchase of feminist ideas if we cannot understand why so many women read *Woman* and watch *Crossroads*?

Works such as Roland Barthes's *The Pleasure of the Text* (1976) or Laura Mulvey's *Visual Pleasure and Narrative Cinema'* (1975) refer to the psychoanalytic tradition in search of an explanation of specific forms of aesthetic pleasure. It would be easy for exploration of such questions to lapse into subjectivism, and a strength of this approach is that its often fascinating insights are grounded in a theoretical framework that is susceptible to debate and discussion. But some difficulties remain. Laura Mulvey, for instance, demonstrates clearly the voyeurism of narrative film and the ways in which the female body has been objectified for male erotic contemplation, and she concludes that radical film-makers can and should strike a blow against mainstream cinema. 'Women,' she writes, 'cannot view the decline of the traditional film form with anything much more than sentimental regret.' (1975:18). Although this is couched as a likelihood it is in fact a hopeful injunction (not borne out by the ratings for Hollywood movies on the television). Indeed one of the reasons why narrative film is so popular, even among feminists, is that it provides the pleasure so forcibly denied in much radical film. Furthermore, the statement begs an important question which is particularly apposite to this case – what is the nature of the pleasure taken in, precisely, nostalgia and sentimentality? We need to know why the 'women's weepies' have an apparently enduring appeal. It is not enough to declare the impropriety of certain kinds of responses, we need to examine much more open-mindedly and sympathetically their basis in our consciousness and subjectivity.

Conclusion

I began by asking whether, as far as feminist cultural politics is concerned, there is a difference between a work of art and an advertising hoarding. It is often assumed that works of art are like other media of representation in that they are ideological. I have argued that there are dangers in a too extensive politicising of art as ideology: that we should not ignore the fictional, imaginative, aesthetic dimensions of works of art. In short, there are aspects of art that are not reducible to our analytic boxes of ideologies.

To say this is not to insist upon a distinction between popular culture and art. The myths about art and artists must be challenged. A work's status as 'art', and the intentions of 'the artist', do not of themselves construct the meaning of the work. This meaning is socially created in the consumption of the work. (In this sense, although I disputed the claims of *The Dinner Party* to be an *intrinsically* feminist work I would not dispute that it is a feminist event. But this is because its meaning has been constructed, collectively, as such.)

If we emphasize the social construction of meaning in this way, a rigid distinction between art and popular culture will tend to fall away. It may be that works usually defined as art have a higher concentration of non-ideological elements than those thought of as popular culture, the media, or mass communications. But art does not have a monopoly on creativity, skill and imagination. Nor does it have a monopoly on the provision of pleasure. The conventions of particular art forms, through which aesthetic pleasure is mediated, have their counterparts in the conventions specific to particular forms of popular culture. The mechanical models of ideology, and the desperate resort to notions of 'false-consciousness', are adequate for understanding neither. Cultural politics, and feminist art, are important precisely because we are not the helpless victims of oppressive ideology. We take some responsibility for the cultural meaning of gender and it is up to us all to change it. But this struggle cannot rest on a challenge to ideological dimensions of the old-master painting – it will also have to engage with the aesthetic pleasures of advertisements.

This paper is based on a talk given at the Communist University of London, 1980. For comments on a written draft I would like to thank Rosalind Coward, Mary McIntosh, Kay Syrad, Michelene Wandor, Janet Wolff and the editors of this volume.

References

Barthes, Roland, *The Pleasure of the Text*, Cape, London, 1976.

Brontë, Charlotte, *Shirley*, Dent, London, 1965.

Coward, Rosalind, 'Are Women's Novels Feminist Novels?' *Feminist Review* No 5 1980.

Mulvey, Laura, 'Visual Pleasure and Narrative Cinema', *Screen*, Vol. 16, No.3, Autumn 1975.

Showalter, Elaine, 'Towards a Feminist Poetics', in Mary Jacobus (ed.), *Women Writing and Writing about Women*, Croom Helm, London, 1979.

Williams, Raymond, *Culture*, Fontana, London, 1981.

Wolff, Janet, *The Social Production of Art*, Macmillan, London, 1981.

'Mothers, Vote Labour!' The State, the Labour Movement and Working-Class Mothers, 1900-1918

Caroline Rowan

You may not know it, Baby dear, but the Great Ones of the land are thinking and talking of you today ... When they say 'Look after Baby!' they know not what that means. It means a new Britain, my kid, it means more room to live, more light, more air, more wages for your Mother and your Dad, it means a very different world from the world we're saddled with today (*Labour Woman*, September 1915).

These words were written by women in the Labour Party at a time when, with a few tentative reforms, the foundations were being laid for what we now know as the welfare state. The quotation illustrates the battle constantly being fought between classes over the form and content of welfare. To the 'Great Ones' of the land, it meant little more than education in the correct form of child-rearing. To the working-class authors of that article, it meant something much wider: access to material resources and an improvement in the quality of working-class life.

This dilemma is still with us today and features centrally in Marxist debates on the nature of the welfare state. The struggle between competing definitions illustrated in the above quotation makes it clear that accounts which see welfare as either serving the needs of capital (Saville, 1957), or as hard-won gains for the working-class (Thompson, 1958) are grossly oversimplified. More recent definitions, such as Poulantzas' account of the state as a 'point of condensation' whose form is determined by the balance of social forces in struggle

(Poulantzas, 1978), go further towards understanding the complexity of welfare. It is important to recognize, first, that both major classes have an interest in the welfare of the working class, and second, that the form and content of welfare legislation is the outcome of political struggle. The value of welfare services to the capitalist and working class respectively depends both on the overall balance of political forces and the level and form of working-class mobilization around a particular issue. This has the important effect of assigning a key role to working-class struggle in determining the nature of welfare services.

Marxist feminists have been concerned to extend this approach to include gender relations. The main problem here is that gender divisions exist both within and between classes. Although it is usually the case that capitalism and patriarchy reinforce one another in a given social formation, this cannot always be assumed. For example, some welfare measures might be in the interests of capitalism and working-class women, but not of working-class men. We cannot therefore assume a natural alliance between capitalism and patriarchy on the one hand and socialism and feminism on the other.

In addition, the differential power relations between men and women have led to tensions between socialists and feminists in the labour movement. The object of this article is to explore these tensions and the ways in which women in the labour movement have negotiated them.

If one regards the family as a key site of patriarchal power relations, albeit as a result of historical development, rather than biological inevitability, then state intervention in the family can be seen as the point of intersection of class and gender struggle and the point at which tensions and contradictions between the two are likely to be most evident. This is why I have chosen this topic.

The early twentieth century, particularly the 1906-11 Liberal Government, saw a proliferation of welfare reforms. Many historians (see for example J.R.Hay, 1975) see in these reforms the origins of the modern welfare state; this is why this period is the focus of the article.

The new legislation included the introduction of unemployment and sickness insurance and old age pensions.

These can be broadly located in the context of an economic and political crisis in which Britain was threatened, from without, by industrial competition from France, Germany and the USA, and, from within, by the growing strength of the labour movement. They may therefore be seen as political concessions to contain working-class militancy, and, in some cases, as attempts to solve the economic crisis by improving the quality of labour power. This problem was particularly acute in the light of technological changes which demanded a more skilled, stable and healthy labour force, and the general need to rationalize production in order to compete internationally.

It was the problem of labour power that led to intensified state concern with the working-class family, particularly with working-class women and children. The scandalously high level of infant mortality and poor physique of the survivors revealed the extent to which labour power was being squandered at its source. Awareness of this was intensified by the Boer War at the beginning of the period and the First World War at the end, both of which compounded the problem by the need for healthy soldiers, and also revealed Britain's inadequacies in comparison with her imperial rivals. This was particularly true of the Boer War, when many of the recruits were found to be unfit for service.

The resulting legislation focused on child health and the conditions of child-rearing and procreation. It included the 1902 Registration of Midwives Act, which aimed to prohibit midwifery by untrained persons, and some limited provision for maternity benefit under the 1911 National Insurance Act. School meals and school medical inspection were introduced in 1906 and 1907 respectively. In addition, local authorities were encouraged to set up infant consultations or welfare centres and schools for mothers, with the aid of central government grants, made available from the Board of Education in 1907 and the Local Government Board (LGB) in 1914. These schemes were greatly expanded after the LGB grant and accompanying circular to local authorities, outlining a model scheme, consolidated in the 1918 Maternity and Child Welfare Act.

A few infant welfare centres provided basic medical treatment, milk and meals for nursing mothers and sterilized milk for bottle-fed infants, but the general aim of consultations, schools and welfare centres was to instruct the mother in child-rearing. The child's ill health was regarded as a product of the mother's ignorance, rather than material conditions, such as poverty, poor housing or bad sanitation. The labour movement was crucial in the struggle for the recognition of material causes, particularly as the position of organized labour was strengthened by the First World War. It is therefore essential to examine the degree to which the specific needs of women were taken up.

The development of family legislation raised broader issues which had major implications for the work of men and women in the labour movement. First, the general question of parental responsibility as against state provision for children, particularly in the case of school meals, raised the question of whether the ideal socialist form of childcare was the individual family or more collective, state-controlled responsibility. A related question was that of women's respective roles as mothers and wage earners. Thirdly, occurring as it did in the context of a long history of philanthropic, and also (via the Poor Law) state, intrusions into the working-class family, child welfare legislation was bound to be regarded with some suspicion as yet another attempt to impose alien norms on the working-class family. We need to consider the effect of this suspicion on working-class mobilization and also the extent to which it was justified. In the long term, were the regulative aspects of the legislation outweighed by a real improvement in the material conditions of working-class family life and particularly in the status of women within the working-class family?

The Labour Movement and Ideologies of the Family

In stressing the importance of working-class mobilization around specific issues, we need to examine not only the ideological constraints on working-class mobilization, but also the initiatives that were taken in relation to the potential for working-class intervention, within the overall balance of forces.

Labour mobilization round welfare issues should be seen against the background of a limited suffrage, which still excluded many working-class men and all women, and a relatively weak Parliamentary Labour Party. For most of the period, therefore, the main scope for labour activity was extra-parliamentary struggle. The non-statutory nature of the legislation meant that whether and how it was implemented depended on progressive forces putting pressure on local authorities in their area. It was, however, usually public health officials, rather than labour activists, who led the fight for local implementation. Bradford was the exception which proved the rule. A strong labour group on the council, backed up by consistent local public campaigning, forced the early implementation of school meals and municipal maternity schemes.

The struggle for the implementation of welfare legislation was waged alongside the struggle for its extension. Since the latter involved decisions about the form and content of welfare, the nature of the working-class demands was crucial. Insofar as they campaigned for the improvement of material conditions, rather than just medical inspection, diagnosis and advice, labour activists did much to dispel the myth of maternal ignorance. Nevertheless, a concerted labour mobilization was constantly impeded by deep ideological divisions as to the ideal socialist form of child-rearing. In the words of Margaret MacMillan, an ILP member and leading child welfare campaigner, in both Bradford and London:

> Some ... are eager to withdraw children from their home surroundings and place them in schools, where they will be trained, bathed, dressed and equipped for life under competent teachers and attendants; while others, such as Mr Blatchford, are opposed to schools and formal education altogether and declare that home is the only training ground and that the only head-teacher should be the mother. All this is a little confusing to the rank and file socialist, and, what is more, it leaves him under a vague impression that this is one of the many subjects on which he need not, for the present at least, make up his mind (*The Child and the State*, 1911, p.1).

At one end of the spectrum, the Social Democratic Federation (SDF) claimed that the rearing of the next generation was a communal, not an individual duty. They therefore advocated school feeding as part of a wider scheme of state maintenance, which included the removal of children to boarding-schools outside the towns. An enlightened education in healthy and artistic surroundings would aim, not to 'cram', but to 'give the children well-developed bodies and minds, so as to equip them more thoroughly for later life' (*Social Democrat*, June 1905). They would also learn collective citizenship and 'the solidarity of the human race' (*Social Democrat*, June 1900). State maintenance would not mean the removal of control and responsibility from working-class parents. Parental responsibility would be exercised collectively rather than individually:

> If the state took over the maintenance of the children, it would still be the workers who would really feed them, clothe them and build the good boarding schools which we would like to see by the seaside, on the sandy wastes and in the great open spaces (J. Hunter Watts at National Labour Conference, 1905).

The SDF was the only revolutionary party of any significance in the British labour movement, and it was doubtless its conception of the need for a revolutionary break with present conditions which enabled it to envisage such radically different forms of childcare. SDF policy should not, however, be dismissed as infantile leftism. It was based less on the narrow dogmatism of its leaders than on attempts to apply their theory at local level. Their extensive grassroots experience dated back to the School Boards in the 1880s and voluntary feeding schemes in which SDF branches were prominent in the 1890s.

In advocating communal, rather than privatized childcare, they were nonetheless in a minority in the labour movement. Their case was forcefully put at the National Labour Conference on the State Maintenance of Children, in January 1905, in the organization of which they were prominent. Ramsay MacDonald organized a rival event, through the Labour Representation Committee. This was explicitly on the Provision of School Meals, and an amendment on state maintenance was heavily defeated. A similar amendment at the 1909 Labour Party Conference was defeated by 712,000 votes to 248,000.

Katherine Bruce Glazier, a leading member of the

Independent Labour Party, took up cudgels against state maintenance in a pamphlet *Socialism and the Home*, published by the ILP in 1911. She praised the emotional warmth of the nuclear family and claimed that state maintenance, rather than home maintenance of children, was 'alien to the whole history, hope and spirit of socialism'.

The defence of the individual family was indeed part of a tradition in British socialist thought, a tradition which owed much to Morris and Ruskin and in which the nuclear family was part of a rural community which had been destroyed by the Industrial Revolution. It is no coincidence that Keir Hardie, and many others, spoke of the restoration of true motherhood and a return to nature in the same breath, stating at a Women's Labour League Conference, that he:

> did not believe in any substitute for the child's mother, nor did he believe in the gymnasium as a substitute for the forest as the training ground of the normal youngster (*Women's Labour League*, 1912).

Like the SDF the ILP blamed industrialisation for the disruption of working-class family life. Their solution, however, was the reestablishment of a lost rural idyll, into which mother fitted as naturally as the English forest (and probably had as much control over her own destiny.)

Child welfare measures were therefore regarded by many in the Labour Party and trade-union movement as temporary palliatives, pending the restoration of the family 'on a sound economic foundation' (J.R. MacDonald, 1909). It was not easy to fight with conviction for mere palliatives, the more so as the theoretical differences within the labour movement were inextricably linked to the question of the family wage. This was partly a tactical argument, which would give not only maximum wages but also greater control than any form of services in kind to the individual wage earner. However, its close connection with the underlying ideological differences is brought out by the fact that only the SDF countered the argument that services in kind would depress wages with the reply that this would not matter:

The individual worker whose wages had fallen by the amount he had previously spent on feeding his children would know that they were better fed and maintained than at home, and he would know also that in times of strike and unemployment they would not suffer (J. Hunter Watts, at National Labour Conference).

The question of the labour movement's defence of the family wage has been analysed by Michèle Barrett and Mary McIntosh (1980). They point out that the ideology which relegates women to the home and gives the male wage earner the responsibility for economically supporting the whole family has never in practice led to higher wages for the working class, while it *has* increased the subordination of women and led to divisions between men and women in the labour movement. They also stress that the labour movement must take responsibility for this development:

> the relegation of women to the home cannot be explained solely with reference to the "needs of Capitalism" but was the object of struggle, *and therefore choice*, of the working class (pp. 53-4, my emphasis).

While their choice was doubtless partly determined by men's misconceived economic interest, it was also partly due to their patriarchal interest in an institution where they were privileged, both economically, having total control of the family income, and by virtue of being serviced by their wives, even when the latter were also involved in some form of waged work. This does not, of course, mean that all working-class men abused their wives. There is, in fact, considerable evidence that most working-class men handed over their wages to their wives to 'lay out' the family budget. It does, however, mean that the tendency of the class as a whole was to defend the status quo, in which men were *structurally* in a position of power over women.

The implications of the family wage for labour movement strategy were most apparent in the opposition of the Labour Party and later the TUC to any form of economic independence for wives and mothers, whether through wage earning or through the state endowment of motherhood. On other forms of child welfare legislation, they tended to be indifferent, rather than oppositional. The provision of intermittent medical treatment, including milk and food, was a gain that was unlikely to be offset by a loss in wages. Moreover, the advice offered to working-class women in welfare centres reinforced, rather than challenged, their role in the domestic sphere. However, even here, agreement was struggled for over many years, and it was not until the First World War that the movement's ambivalence, shown in the debates about school meals and state maintenance, was finally overcome.

The impetus for this came mainly from the women's organizations, and I shall therefore examine in some detail the Women's Cooperative Guild (WCG) and the Women's Labour League (WLL). There was considerable overlap both in aims and membership between these organizations. They differed in emphasis, rather than purpose. Nevertheless, at the risk of exaggerating their differences, I want to consider them separately, because their different approaches often reflected deeper ideological differences. I shall try to locate their activities round welfare legislation in the broader context of their overall structure and aims, and particularly the extent of their autonomy from their 'brother' organisations.

The Women's Cooperative Guild

The WCG was founded in 1883 with the aim of securing for the women – 'the housekeepers and shoppers of the nation' – greater decision-making powers within the Cooperative movement. Probably because of its close connection with a movement mainly concerned with distribution, rather than production, its membership consisted of wives and mothers, rather than women employed in industry.

By 1919 it had approximately 32,000 members and membership continued to rise between the wars to over 50,000. The personal influence of its Secretary, Margaret Llewelyn Davies, was considerable. She held office from 1889 to 1921. With her Christian Socialist background, university education and early experience as a sanitary inspector, she was determined from the start that the Guild should go beyond immediate domestic concerns to practical social reform.

However, this required considerable positive discrimination and special political education for women. The Guild recognized this and held classes in book-keeping and public speaking for members and officials. It emphasised above all that women would learn most from the experience of organizing their own activity and, in this context, autonomy from the Cooperative Societies was crucial:

> How, if men took part in the work, would the great mass of the members overcome their shyness about speaking in public, or take their full part in organizing the work? (*Special education, divorce and independence*, in Harris Collection).

Self-government was important in asserting women's rights within the Cooperative movement, for example in the long struggle for 'Open membership', which would enable wives of Cooperators to hold shares in their own right. This was heavily opposed in some Societies, such as Chatham, where it was resisted for nine years, before its final acceptance in 1906.

The autonomy of the Guild affected not only its strength within the Cooperative movement, but also the content of its political activity. It prided itself on being on the 'progressive side' of the Cooperative movement, and showed a greater concern with social questions, rather than the narrower aspects of cooperative trading. For example it favoured the extension of cooperation to the poor, an idea regarded with suspicion by most Societies, which tended to be rather exclusive savings schemes for the artisan and lower middle classes (Cole, 1944). The Guild also advocated the use of profits for communal facilities, rather than individual dividend, and fought long and hard for decent pay and conditions for Cooperative employees.

The most celebrated example of the Guild's assertion of its autonomy was its progressive submission to the Royal Commission on Divorce, which so angered the movement's Catholic supporters that in 1914 the Central Board of the Cooperative Union withdrew its annual grant of £400 to the Guild. It was not just divorce law reform, but the political autonomy of the Guild that was at issue, and the Guild stood its ground until the Central Board capitulated unconditionally in 1918 – the year in which women's suffrage suddenly made them desirable allies.

Lifting the curtain – the Maternity Campaign

The Guild's stress on social reform did not mean that the private sphere of the home was ignored. On the contrary, Miss Davies stressed that the dichotomy between women's public and private lives was a false one:

> In the past, a heavy curtain had, on marriage, fallen on a woman's life, and the nation felt no responsibility for her personal welfare and the conditions under which she performed her great tasks (*Special education*).

This was most apparent in the campaign for the national care of maternity. The Guild campaigned vigorously for provision for married non-wage-earning women and the payment of maternity benefit in the 1911 Insurance Act, and urged that maternity benefit should be paid direct to the mother. It achieved this when the Act was amended in 1913, despite the opposition of Labour MPs, both at the Committee stage and in the final Commons vote.

It was its firm belief in married women's right to economic independence which enabled the Guild to mount such a concerted campaign on this issue. A resolution passed at the 1911 Annual Conference states its position:

> Seeing that the wife contributes by her work in the home to the maintenance of the family equally with her husband, this Conference is of the opinion that wives should be recognized as joint heads of household and that some form of economic independence should be legally assured to them (1910-11 Annual Report).

In the light of this the payment of maternity benefit direct to mothers was particularly significant:

> It was the first public recognition of the mother's place in the home, and a new step towards some economic independence for wives (1913-14 Annual Report).

The Guild also campaigned consistently for a comprehensive

national scheme of maternity care. This was put before Lord Rhondda at the Local Government Board in a detailed memorandum in 1917. It was based on free and universal provision, without any taint of the Poor Law or charity, and included a universal public health maternity allowance, skilled medical attention on confinement, maternity homes and convalescent homes for normal deliveries, and access to public hospitals for more complicated cases, trained home helps during confinement, and local maternity centres, which would provide simple medical treatment, including milk and meals for mother and infant, if necessary. Unified central administration by one government department was essential, and this led to the demand for a Ministry of Health, which should have a Maternity and Infant Welfare Department, mainly staffed by women. Locally, administration should be by municipal maternity committees, which should be made compulsory for all local authorities, because, for married women who had no municipal vote, they were the only available form of representation. The Guild insisted strongly on the representation of working women on these committees and that the work should be municipal and not philanthropic in character:

> Members of the Guild feel strongly that 'ladies' who have sat on charitable committees may be out of touch with the point of view of independent working women (1917 Memo).

In its campaigning, the Guild combined parliamentary lobbying with good publicity work and easily mobilized local organization. For example its success in the campaign for maternity benefit to be paid to the mother was largely due to a 'lightning campaign' in which over seven hundred signatures were collected from local public health and sanitary officials, nursing associations, Guardians and councillors, in less than a week.

It was in the localities that the real strength of the Guild lay. In line with its stress on working women's involvement in municipal maternity committees, the 1914-15 Annual Report record the membership of fifty Guildswomen of such committees. For 1915-16, the figure is forty-four, for 1916-1' seventy-five, for 1917-18 259 and for 1918-19 184. These figures are even more striking when compared with the Women's Labour League, who record no figures at all until 1917-18, when it had only 31 members active on maternity committees. In addition, Guild branches campaigned for the local implementation of legislation, where municipal maternity committees did not exist. In 1914-15, for example, 102 branches in 82 towns organized conferences of local women's organizations on the subject.

There is little evidence of attempts to set up alternative Cooperative maternity centres parallel with municipal services. Babies' Dispensaries were widely discussed in 1906-7 and a paper was produced which recommended Cooperative Health Departments and particularly stressed the glaring need for medical provision for women and children. This was in line with the Guild's policy of collective, rather than individual appropriation of Cooperative profits. However, the danger of bypassing the municipal authority was emphasized:

> A close alliance should be maintained between our Health Department and the Health Committee of the Town Council, for the work of each would be largely complementary (WCG, 1907).

Thus, Cooperative Health Departments may have foundered partly on the conservatism of the Cooperative Societies, clinging to their divi, but it is clear that the WCG also realised even at this relatively early stage the importance of municipal and state responsibility for motherhood.

By far the most spectacular aspect of the WCG Maternity campaign was the publication in 1915 of *Maternity: Letters from Working Women*. The letters described Guild members' experiences of pregnancy and childbirth. Purely in terms of publicity, the book was a success; by 1916, it was in its third edition and had been reviewed by *The Times, Daily News, Manchester Guardian, New Statesman, Yorkshire Post, British Medical Journal, Votes for Women* and *Labour Leader*. Its catalogue of mental and physical suffering made for harrowing, often stomach-churning reading, and its forthright exposure of the physical risks involved in childbirth for the working classes must have been a startling revelation to those in more comfortable circumstances.

However, the importance of the book went well beyond its publicity value. Unlike other work on child-rearing at this time, the book focused on the mother's wellbeing, rather than the problem of infant mortality. This was consistent with Miss Davies's own repeated emphasis on 'the mother's side of the question', and the women correspondents themselves also saw the problem in terms of their own rights. While there was no lack of concern for their children, they were free from the cloying romanticism of motherhood and stressed the mental and physical strain on their own health: the well-founded fear of death in childbirth, the permanent injury which often followed a difficult labour and the perpetual worry of making ends meet.

Even more important was the book's role in 'lifting the curtain' on the lives of married working-class women. For the first time, it was recognized that their experience not only mattered, but should be publicly discussed. In the Introduction, Miss Davies described how the isolation of women in the home had hitherto prevented 'any common expression of their needs'. The result of this common expression was the discovery that women's suffering was by no means inevitable and the formulation of a comprehensive political programme to avoid it.

This programme, outlined at the end of the book and broadly similar to the one put before Lord Rhondda in 1917, was carefully formulated in the light of the experience of the women themselves. For example, housework was recognized as necessary and demanding labour and the injury which resulted from taking up household duties too soon after a confinement is a recurring theme in the book.

The book was also unique in demanding reforms from men, as well as the state. Miss Davies stressed in the Introduction:

> In plain language, both in law and popular morality, the wife is still the inferior of the husband.

With the exception of one fascinating letter in *Labour Woman* (February 1919), I have found little evidence of discussion of personal relationships elsewhere in the labour movement. This letter deserves attention, precisely because it is so exceptional.

It contains ten rules for husbands, which range from choosing a house with a bright outlook from the kitchen, a good copper and cooking stove, to helping with heavy housework, making sure his wife has time to read the literature of the Labour Party and church and taking it in turn to attend meetings. However, apart from this one lonely (and anonymous) feminist, the WCG stood alone in tackling personal relationships between husband and wife.

The Guild was even more alone in discussing not only personal, but also sexual relations. Some of the letters were in advance of public opinion in advocating birth control and condoning abortion, while others demanded male sexual abstinence to avoid continual pregnancy:

> But no amount of State help can help the suffering of mothers until men are taught many things in regard to the right use of the organs of reproduction, and until he realises that the wife's body belongs to herself, and until the marriage relations takes a higher sense of morality and bare justice (WCG, 1978).

G.D.H. Cole (Cole, 1944) rightly attributed the Guild's success to its intimate knowledge of its members' daily lives. However, to leave it at this would imply that the Guild recognized the problems of involving housewives in politics and so limited its campaigns to domestic issues. The Guild went beyond this to formulate some of the most advanced political demands of the period and to achieve the implementation of a fair proportion of them. This can only be explained by its emphasis on the twin principles of democracy and autonomy, which enabled it to formulate its political beliefs on the basis of shared experience and fight for them with confidence. Its strong sense of autonomy enabled it to confront the implications of an analysis which recognized not only the inequalities between classes but also those between men and women and to oppose the latter both inside and outside the labour movement.

The Women's Labour League

The WLL was founded in 1906 and remained in existence until 1918 when it was replaced by the Labour Party Women's sections. It was, from the outset, closely associated with the Labour Party in aims and organization. Its leaders, Margaret Bondfield, Marion Phillips, Margaret MacDonald and Mary MacArthur, were all prominent in Labour Party politics. There is little evidence of conflict with the Labour Party, either over the autonomy of the League or on questions of policy. On contentious issues, Labour Party policy usually prevailed in the League.

The League stressed that its aim was not separation from, but closer cooperation with Labour men. The need for separate organization of women was seen solely in terms of compensatory political education, to enable them to play a fuller role in the Labour Party as a whole. They recognized the specific needs of women, arising from their primary role as wives and mothers, but, while it would be unfair to say that the rights of women as houseworkers were neglected, the main emphasis was on their contribution as wives and mothers. Reversing the priorities of the WCG, which were to transcend domestic responsibility to 'the world beyond the family and even beyond the store', the League stressed that political activity was necessary for women to carry out their domestic duties fully. As the Report of the Founding Conference put it (June 1906):

> They wanted to show the wives of trades unionists and cooperators particularly ... that the best way to look after their homes was by taking an interest in the life of the community.

This approach developed into a sharp division of labour, a 'separate spheres' argument, in which women's access to political life was premised on their experience and knowledge of the domestic sphere. While this approach put the working conditions of housewives on the political agenda for the first time, it did so in a way that reinforced the existing sexual division of labour. Women's role was often described as to 'bring the mother-spirit into politics', thus linking their domestic role to their more 'caring' natures. While this produced more rhetoric about women's superiority, its radical potential, namely its explicit critique of masculinity, was blunted by its containment within labourism. By carrying the existing sexual division of labour over into organized politics conflict within the labour movement was avoided over such issues as women's position in the labour force or the family wage.

Women's economic independence was probably the most hotly debated issue in the League's history, precisely because it challenged the division between male breadwinner and female homemaker. It was usually discussed in relation to three linked questions: the role of mothers in the labour force, protective legislation, and the state endowment of motherhood.

This last was opposed by many in the League, on the grounds that it would lower men's wages, which were theoretically bargained for on the basis of family rather than individual need, and diminish fathers' sense of parental responsibility. This was premissed on the equation of the father's responsibility with financial responsibility, an assumption which also underpinned the opposition of Margaret MacDonald and many others to mothers' engagement in waged work:

> The fact that their wives can supplement the family income has unfortunately had a bad effect on many husbands; it lessens their sense of responsibility as breadwinners. (MacDonald, M. *et al.*, 1909).

Married women's work was also discouraged because 'the home was the heart of the nation and there could be no home life for the child where the mother went to the factory'. (Annual Report 1909-10.)

However, these assumptions were not unchallenged, particularly in the early days of the League. The opposition received a powerful impetus from the Fabian Women's Group (FWG) who at this stage worked closely with the Central London branch of the WLL. They argued strongly for married women's right to work and the state endowment of motherhood as a step towards the payment of an individual, rather than a family wage, in order to break women's economic dependence on men. The publication by the FWG of *Round About a Pound a Week* in 1913, a study of working-class budgets which proved the impossibility of surviving on a male wage alone, provided further substantive arguments in favour of state support.

As the years passed, opinion gradually hardened against women's economic independence. At the 1922 Labour Women's Conference, Mary Stocks, a prominent member of the campaign for family allowances, failed to win conference support for cash allowances paid directly to the mother.

Opinion in the League also hardened against mothers' employment, largely as a result of women's mass involvement in war work. The harsh reality of long hours and unhealthy conditions combined with pressure from the male unions who feared that skilled men's jobs would be lost permanently to the women who replaced them during the war, to produce an intensified ideology of woman's primary role as homemaker. *Women and the Labour Party*, a pamphlet edited by Marion Phillips, which effectively constituted the Labour Party's 1918 election manifesto for women, addressed women mainly as wives and mothers and Mary MacArthur's contribution on *Women as Trades Unionists* made only the most tentative commitment to women's right to paid employment.

Communal facilities, such as municipal kitchens and day nurseries, introduced to facilitate women's war work, produced a contradictory response from Labour women. On the one hand, they were welcomed, because they eased the burden of housework. Marion Phillips, for example, was instrumental in the establishment of municipal kitchens. On the other hand, they were seen as a potential threat to the family unit and an inducement to women to work for wages. This dilemma could only be resolved by a new emphasis on the importance of leisure and intellectual stimulation for women, not primarily in their own interests, but in order to make them better mothers:

> We do not advocate cooperative housekeeping in order that women may work for wages, but because we believe that it may help them to live far healthier and more interesting lives. Mothers as munition workers, as mill hands, do not seem to us any better than mothers as houseworkers, but we do believe that mothers who have time to be thinking citizens would make infinitely better homes for their children than those whose hours are filled with the drudgery of working in overcrowded, inconvenient and ugly homes (Marion Phillips in *Labour Woman*, February 1918).

On the provision of services in kind, (food, medical treatment etc.) there was greater unanimity within the League. They shared the WCG's concern with maternity and infant welfare and ran their own successful Baby Clinic in North Kensington from 1911. The League's main emphasis was on the provision of treatment, as well as advice, and on the need for continuous medical supervision from infancy to adulthood. This led logically, like the WCG's demand for a unified maternity service, to the demand for a Ministry of Health, an issue which united the whole labour movement during the war years.

Neither the demand for a Ministry of Health nor the national concern with maternity were a monopoly of the labour movement and, when it was finally established in 1919, the Ministry was admittedly something of a disappointment, since the administration of maternity benefit and the Poor Law remained outside it. However, it did have a Maternity and Child Welfare Department, staffed by six women doctors, and for this the labour movement in general and Labour women in particular can take considerable credit.

It was during the First World War that the WLL's close links with the labour movement became an asset. As organized labour became more powerful, due to its centrality to the war effort, Labour women also gained influence. The War marked the beginning of a new tendency for women to work with, or even within government. Several women were appointed to government committees, such as the Central Committee on Women's Employment, the Consumer Council's Sub Committee on Municipal Kitchens and the Women's Housing Advisory Committee of the Ministry of Reconstruction. None of these were important committees in themselves, but they did mark a new direction for the work of Labour Women. The Housing Committee was the most important, since its brief was to examine plans for post-war housing 'with specific reference to the convenience of the housewife'. This enabled Labour women to put the question of housework not just on the political agenda of the left, but on the agenda of the policy makers themselves.

Close cooperation with organized labour also paid off in terms of changing labour movement attitudes towards women. This was most apparent in the War Emergency: National Workers' Committee (WE:WNC), a labour movement body set up in August 1914 to defend working-class interests in wartime. Its Executive Committee had five women members and it actively promoted maternal and child welfare, both by encouraging local labour activity for the implementation of existing legislation (particularly on school meals and maternity schemes) and by urging on the government new measures, like priority for pregnant women and young children in the allocation of the national milk supply, increased separation allowances, municipal kitchens to help working women and better treatment for unmarried mothers.

That this was not a temporary wartime phenomenon was shown by the fact that a government attempt to economize in 1921 by reducing grants for the local authority provision of milk for mothers and children was defeated by a prompt and well-organized labour movement campaign.

The strong wording of a resolution from the Standing Joint Council of Industrial Women's Organizations shows the extent to which state provision for maternity had become accepted in the labour movement:

> That this Committee affirms that the care of infants and mothers is a primary duty of the state; it protests against any reduction of those services, and in particular against any reduction of the supply of milk to infants and expectant mothers (*Labour Woman*, February 1922).

This transformation can only be attributed to the hard work of women active in labour organizations.

Conclusion

Returning to our initial formulation of the welfare state as an arena of class and gender struggle, we need to do two things: first, to examine the overall balance of forces and the extent to which labour movement demands were met in welfare services achieved to the working class, women and capital.

For the reasons outlined in the introduction, the early twentieth century was a period conducive to welfare legislation, particularly in relation to the family. It was also a period of increasing labour strength, so that much depended on the attitude of the labour movement to family legislation. Despite some fundamental divisions, labour resistance to state intervention in the family was substantially weakened, particularly after 1914, at least in respect of provision in kind. This was due to a number of factors: the successful operation of school meals without disastrous consequences for family life, the general trend towards collective provision in wartime, and women's independence as a result of the war and their increasing political 'value' as potential voters; it was also due to the activity and pressure of the labour women's organizations which developed in the period.

Of these, the WCG and the WLL were the most important. They should be seen as complementary. The greater autonomy of the WCG enabled it to go further in fighting for women's rights, particularly in relation to maternity benefit, but it was backed up on all other issues by the WLL, whose close organizational links with the Labour Party and trade unions compensated to some extent for its lack of autonomy, and enabled it to teach Labour men about women's issues.

Among the successes, we can count the establishment of a Ministry of Health. Despite its limitations, some progress was made towards a unified public health service, and the principle of state responsibility for health was established. Although there was still no compulsion on local authorities to provide child welfare facilities, heightened public awareness of the problem, central government grants and pressure from the Ministry meant that many of them did so. As we have seen, some gains, such as infants' milk, were even defended in the face of the governement economy cuts of 1921-2.

The struggle for the endowment of motherhood was less successful. This was due, in part, to the strong vested interests of the insurance companies, who ensured that maternity benefit remained insurance based, rather than a universal right. However, an additional factor was undoubtedly the ambivalence of the labour movement towards women's economic independence, which was clearly motivated by patriarchal interests and prevented a cohesive mobilization in favour of universal maternity benefit.

If the endowment of motherhood was defeated, largely because of divisions in the labour movement, to what do we attribute its success? It was the women's organizations who took the initiative and their success was mainly due to their careful formulation of demands and strategies, in a way which guaranteed the best possible outcome for working-class women. There were two main dangers: that welfare services would be conceded as charity and that they would take the form of the imposition of alien middle-class norms on working-class families. These problems were solved, not by an abstentionist rejection of the services offered, but by stressing that these services were a right, to be administered by the state, not by charity, and that ill health had material, not moral causes, which required material resources, not pious advice, for its prevention and cure.

The fight for the involvement of the working-class women in the administration of welfare services was also crucial in avoiding philanthropic intrusions. The dogged insistence of the WCG, and later the WLL, on working women's representation on municipal maternity committees was so effective that the LGB Circular explaining the 1915 Notification of Births (Extension) Act said of local committees:

> In any such committee it will be desirable to include working women, who might with advantage be representatives of women's organisations. Where no local women's organisation exists, some central organisation might possibly assist by suggesting suitable women (quoted in WCG, 1978).

Central to this strategy was the assertion of the validity of working-class experience. Time and again, progressive working-class women asserted the importance of counterposing working-class experience to scientific expertise – whether on maternity committees or in housing. Nevertheless, experience was not an unproblematic category for labour movement women. While its validity had to be asserted against constant attempts to impose alien norms on working-class family life, it often represented conservative prejudice and reinforced the patriarchal structure of the working-class family itself. Women in the labour movement walked a permanent tight-rope between defending working-class autonomy and 'educating' working-class women to more progressive ideas.

The tension between the validity of working-class

experience and its tendency to conservatism was at its sharpest in relation to debates about private and communal facilities. The desire for privacy must be seen in the context of generations of forced communal living in overcrowded tenements. The failure to challenge traditional family lifestyles was doubtless an element, but so too was the tradition of privacy as a working-class defence against poverty.

Progressive women's organizations had constantly to distinguish between reasonable demands for privacy and individuality (such as dislike of the communal washhouse) and instinctive prejudice which impeded progress. This could only be done with the greatest sensitivity and in full consultation with the working-class women concerned.

Close acquaintance with working women's daily lives enabled Labour and Cooperative women to formulate demands that guaranteed the best possible outcome in relation to their real needs. Perhaps the best example is the WLL's Housing Campaign, which unfortunately lies outside the scope of this article, but the WCG's comprehensive maternity scheme and the WLL's insistence on material provision, food and medical treatment as well as advice, are further relevant examples.

In discussing the specific formulation of demands by working-class women, we are already moving into our final area of discussion: the value of welfare services to working-class women. There was, in my view, a coincidence of interests between capital, in improving the health and efficiency of future workers, and working-class women, in reducing infant mortality and improving their children's health. It is arguable that child welfare facilities were not extensive enough and might have been more extensive with strong labour movement support, but it is in my view indisputable that such facilities as were provided led to an improvement in working-class living standards, a decline in infant mortality and fewer burdens on the working-class housewife. This was the case, largely because working-class women fought hard to minimize the 'educative' approach to child welfare and demanded as a right the material necessities for raising healthy children: decent housing, medical treatment and freedom from poverty.

It is undeniable, as Anna Davin (1978) and Carol Dyhouse (1978) argue, that state intervention in the working-class family did establish new norms of mothering, which trapped the mother more firmly in a web of domestic responsibility. The state now addressed the mother directly on matters concerning the health of her child, instead of through the male head of the household as before. Her duties as a mother were more closely specified and she was answerable, not to an individual patriarch, but to legal, administrative and educative institutions, heavily informed by patriarchal ideology. Middle-class intrusions into the working-class home probably did not increase overall, but the new health visitors, midwives and medical officers were experts better able to initiate specific skills and values than their amateur philanthropic predecessors. The working-class family thus became more efficiently geared to capitalism's need for a healthy, disciplined labour force. In this sense, we may talk with justice of a shift in the patriarchal centre of gravity, from the individual family to the political and ideological levels.

However, this in itself took the struggle onto a different plane. The working-class home was opened up, not only to closer state regulation, but also as a legitimate sphere of political struggle. If child-rearing and housewifery were civic duties, they could demand civic rights in return. The FWG recognized this, in its repeated emphasis on the link between the importance of motherhood and votes for women. The WLL also recognized it, in their campaigns for decent living conditions for working-class women, but they never went beyond demanding the means to fulfil their duty adequately. The WCG at the time, and others in the future, could build on this and demand improved conditions for women in their own right. For example, the campaign against infant mortality was succeeded in the thirties by campaigns against maternal mortality and injury in childbirth (see Lewis, 1980). The Women's Health Enquiry (Rice 1939) followed naturally from the WLL's housing campaign of the Reconstruction period. The campaign for birth control gained momentum in the inter-war years and there was a greater concern with women's health generally. None of this would have been possible without the crucial first steps taken in this period to destroy the notion of the absolute privacy of the family and put the personal health of women and children on the political agenda.

I should like to thank all those who have helped me with comments and discussion, especially: Sue Bruley, Anna Davin, Tricia Davis, Martin Durham, Richard Johnson, Jane Lewis, Bill Schwarz.

Bibliography

Barrett, M. and McIntosh, M. 'The "Family Wage" – Some Problems for Socialists and Feminists' in *Capital and Class* (no. 2, 1980).

Bruce Glazier K., *Socialism and the Home* (1911).

Cole, G.D.H., *A Century of Cooperation* (1944).

Davin, A., 'Imperialism and Motherhood' in *History Workshop Journal*, no. 5. (Spring, 1978).

Dyhouse, C., 'Working Class Mothers and Infant Mortality in England 1895-1914', in *Journal of Social History* (Winter 1978).

Harris Collection, *WCG Archive Collection*, donated to LSE Library (1882-1921).

Hay, J.R., *The Origin of the Liberal Welfare Reforms 1906-14* (1975).

Labour Woman (1913-22), previously the *League Leaflet* (1911-12).

Lewis, J., *The Politics of Motherhood: Child and Maternal Welfare in England 1900-1939.* (1980)

MacDonald, J.R., *Socialism and Government* (1909).

MacDonald, M. et al.: *Wage-earning mothers* (?1909)

MacMillan, M., *The Child and the State.* (1911)

National Labour Conference on the State Maintenance of Children, 20 January 1905, Report of Proceedings.

Phillips, M. (ed), *Women and the Labour Party* (1918).

Poulantzas, N., 'The welfare state, an historical approach', in *New Reasoner* (Autumn 1957).

Reeves, M. Pember, *Round about a Pound a Week* (1913; reprinted by Virago 1979).

Rice, M. Spring, *Working Class Wives: their health and conditions* (1939; reprinted by Virago 1981).

Social Democrat (June 1900, June 1905).

Saville, J., 'The welfare state, an historical approach' in *New Reasoner*, (Autumn 1957).

Thompson, D., 'Discussion: the welfare state', in *New Reasoner* (Spring 1958).

W Emergency: Workers' National Committee: *Minutes of the Executive Committee* (1914-18)

Women's Cooperative Guild (WCG): Annual Reports (1893-1919)

WCG, *Health Departments in connection with Cooperative Societies,* paper for Annual Conference (1907).

WCG, *Maternity: Letters from Working Women* (1915; reprinted by Virago, 1978)

WCG: *Memorandum on the National Care of Maternity* (1917).

Women's Labour League (WLL): *Annual Reports* (1906-18).

WLL, *The Needs of Little Children* (1912).

'What Kind of Woman is She?' Women and Communist Party Politics, 1941-1955

Tricia Davis

Although feminist historians over the last twelve years have produced an impressive body of work, interest in the forms of women's political organization has so far been limited. This has been partly due to the urgency of developing an adequate analysis of women's oppression, and partly because for many modern feminists the route into the Women's Liberation Movement was through a disenchantment with formal organization as a means of change, and an interest in libertarian alternatives.

However, the current political upheavals and their effects on women have encouraged the Women's Liberation Movement to reexamine a range of questions about organisation and strategy. In the process there has been renewed interest in past movements, particularly their organizations, the social and political conditions under which they struggled, and the circumstances of their victories and defeats.

Of course, such interest is not totally new. For example, Sheila Rowbotham (Rowbotham, 1972) and Barbara Taylor (Taylor, 1979 and 1981) have given consistent attention to forms of feminism in relation to different kinds of socialist organization, a project informed politically by the importance to socialist feminists of making alliances as well as maintaining autonomy.

Much of this work has, however, in various ways, stressed the fit between socialism and feminism. No one could claim that such a fit existed within the Communist Party. There are, though, a number of reasons why I chose to look at women's politics within the Communist Party between 1941 and 1955. First, the Communist Party, despite its smallness relative to other political parties, had a significance beyond its size because of its influence in the trade-union movement and as the arena in which Marxist debates took place. Most important, though, in relation to women, was that whereas the Labour Party was the party of representation, the Communist Party was the party of struggle. The emphasis which the Communist Party gave to mass political activism threw the 'women question' into dramatic relief.

This essay looks at four areas: firstly and briefly at the Communist Party's analysis of women's oppression and the strategic implications drawn from this analysis; secondly, at a further level of connection between Marxist and women's politics which was not always sufficiently recognized by the Communist Party and which, though often at odds with the formal analysis, was nonetheless raised by the party's conception of politics and political activism. This connection was usually made at local grassroots level, but frequently surfaced in debates at congresses and in letters and articles in the party press. In the third section, there is an examination of these two areas in the forties and fifties and the particularly acute tension between them, and finally a discussion of the reasons why, and of the way in which these tensions were contained.

The sharp reaction against women's wartime independence and the return to femininity and domesticity as the prevailing ideology make this a particularly interesting period in this respect. How far was the muting of a militant women's politics due to changes in women's position in society generally? How much was it a result of the current Marxist ideology, and how far did it reflect the inadequacies of the Communist Party's strategy for forming alliances between different interest groups and constituencies?

The underlying argument is that there was no easy or immediate connection between socialism and feminism in the Communist Party of Great Britain between 1941 and 1955. The connections that can be traced were fraught and frequently operated beneath the surface of the party's formal politics.

Moreover, while it is important to focus not only on the important achievement of Communist women in creating a space for themselves and women's issues, it is also important that the questions they raised were ultimately contained and diffused and limited in their political impact.

Communism and Women's Politics: The Theoretical Framework

Since the establishment of a Women's Section in 1924 the Communist Party had always been aware of the need to draw women into political activity. Primarily, however, this interest had been in the importance of women as part of the working class, and the party had found it difficult to extend its analysis of women's oppression beyond a class framework, or, at a practical level, to build meaningful alliances between women from different social strata.

Engels's *Origin of the Family, Private Property and the State* formed the basic text from which a Communist analysis of women's oppression was drawn. A number of extracts from it appeared, along with extracts from the writings of Marx, Lenin, Clara Zetkin and Stalin in *Women and Communism*, a Communist Party reader on the 'the women question' published in 1950. Engels's work linked the subordination of women historically with the rise of private property and class society. On the basis of this connection it followed that women's emancipation could not be achieved through the winning of bourgeois rights, which was seen as the characteristic aim of feminist organizations. Complete equality could only be achieved by the defeat of capitalism.

This analysis was given strategic weight by Lenin and Clara Zetkin (Lenin and Zetkin, 1972). Once capitalist society was overthrown and the workers controlled the means of production and distribution, constitutional inequalities for women could be removed, they thought, and the real task of emancipation – through the socialisation of domestic labour – could begin.

Modern re-readings of Engels (Sacks, 1974 and Delmar, 1976) have rescued him from some of the cruder criticisms which have been levelled against him. In addition, while the failure of the tradition established by Engels to challenge the

sexual division of labour had serious consequences for the
development of a socialist feminist analysis of women's
oppression, Engels himself showed in *The Condition of the Working
Class in England* that he was not unaware of the problem. It is
important to remember, too, that it is only recently, within the
Women's Liberation Movement, that any kind of adequate
alternative to the tradition based on Engels has been developed.
In the thirties, for example, Engels's views and the strategies
developed from them were regarded as progressive even by
feminists like Winifred Holtby. Even in the fifties feminist
writers commended the increased socialisation of domestic
labour, rather than the breakdown of sexual divisions, as the
important precondition of women's emancipation.

However, the strategic implications which were drawn from
Engels and developed by Lenin and Zetkin were decisive in
distancing   Communist   women   from   other   feminist
organizations. Given that women's emancipation could only be
achieved through a socialist revolution, carried out by the
working class and led by a revolutionary party, then women
must be recruited into that party. There was clearly no role for
an autonomous women's movement within this strategic
framework. Although the party recognized that 'women's
special needs and disabilities' might make it necessary to
organize special women's sections in the party and work within
women's groups outside the party, there was concern that
women's groups of whatever kind should contribute to the class
struggle and promote the interests of working-class men as well
as working-class women. Feminism was regarded not only as
bourgeois, but also as divisive of the class. In the last instance, if
not the first, women's place was seen as being shoulder to
shoulder with their men.

Lenin and Zetkin's strategy had been developed in a social
and political situation very different from the British one.
Nevertheless their writings were studied by British Marxists
and their views on the relationship between women and
Communist politics helped to reinforce the suspicion of
feminism already current amongst some of the groups which
came together to form the CPGB in 1920. Socialism and
feminism were presented as mutually antagonistic. Although
by the 1930s, there were women in the CPGB who regarded

themselves as feminists, Communism and feminism entered a long period of mutual mistrust. Whilst this might have been justified on the Communist side by the past record of the Women's Social and Political Union, the most publicly vocal of the suffrage groups, it precluded potentially fruitful alliances with other feminist tendencies, such as the East London Federation of Suffragettes and the Women's Freedom League. It also prevented any dialogue with the National Union of Societies for Equal Citizenship, an influential but openly reformist feminist organization active in the twenties and thirties.

Within the Communist Party itself this mistrust held in abeyance certain questions about the nature of women's subordination and the means of achieving women's emancipation. For whilst the Communist Party of Great Britain, along with other Communist Parties within the international movement, was distancing itself from organized feminism, it was also, inadvertently, raising all kinds of questions which, in retrospect, can be seen as seriously challenging the official Communist position on women's subordination.

Communism and Women's Politics: The Dichotomy

Santiago Carrillo, General Secretary of the Spanish Communist Party, has written that a dichotomy existed in the way in which communist parties operated. This dichotomy went back to the Popular Fronts against fascism in the late thirties, when adherence to the official party line emanating from Moscow inevitably came into conflict with national situations. It was essentially a conflict 'between on the one hand certain of the general ways in which Communist Parties posed the questions – even within what might be called Stalinism with which many of our ideas were imbued – and on the other hand with practice which strove to get to grips with reality and entered into conflict – sometimes one not visible on the surface – with the way in which these questions were posed.' (Carrillo, 1976) While the point he is making is a general one, a dichotomy certainly existed between the official party line on women and some of the ways in which Communist women came, through their politics, to perceive their own situation.

Communism, for example, stressed the importance of extra-parliamentary activity. In the 1951 version of the *British Road to Socialism*, the Communist Party programme, it was envisaged that socialism might be achieved in Britain partly through a transformation of Parliament. However, this was only part of the strategy and *The British Road* recognized that it could neither be achieved, nor succeed in bringing about the transition to socialism without 'a united movement of the people'. Membership of the Communist Party, then, could not, technically speaking at least, simply involve card-carrying and voting, or even sporadic bouts of activity around the time of elections. It had to involve continuous political work, which inevitably raised questions about the difficulties faced by women, especially women with children, in sustaining that level of political activity. It equally raised questions about relationships with men who were politically active according to the exacting demands of the Communist Party. A letter to the *Daily Worker* on 7 May 1947 clearly expressed the dilemma. Signed simply 'A Wife', it read:

> You have some excellent articles in your paper but I have read none so far which describe the so-called Communist who exploits his wife to the hilt. Most working-class wives work in these days of high prices. I for one work from 8 till 6 and have to shop, wash, sew, clean and cook in my spare time. Today I am left laying the oilcloth while 'He' is out shouting 'Down with serfdom.'

Moreover, apart from localized instances of sectarianism, the Communist Party worked consistently not only in the trade unions but also in the broad movements. This last was an especially important area of work for women who were less likely than male Communists to be trade-union activists, but it raised enormous problems of how to work sensitively in a non-Communist organization while at the same time forwarding the party's policies and recruiting to it. Many women handled this well. Others, through no fault of their own, found it difficult and confusing. Certainly, without an adequate political strategy of alliances, success or failure in this area became a very individual matter.

In the forties and fifties the tensions between the party's

theoretical position on women's subordination and those questions within the actual practice of Communist politics became particularly acute. This heightening tension coincided, not accidentally, with an increase of political activity amongst Communist women, both within the party itself and within other organizations.

Through the Doors of Domesticity, 1941-45

Between 1939 and 1941, during the period of the Hitler-Stalin pact, the Communist Party maintained that the war was not a war against fascism but an imperialist war. It gained some support from pacifist groups and more generally for its policies and campaigns around air-raid precautions. This support was expressed in the People's Convention in 1941 and recognized by the Ministry of Information, which was extremely ambivalent about the banning of the *Daily Worker* in January 1941 on the grounds that 'a number of other papers have now taken up the plea for deep shelters ... as well as many other suggestions put forward by the *Daily Worker*' (Memorandum from Mary Adams, director of the Intelligence Division of the Ministry of Information, September 1940). But there were clearly limits to the extent of support for the Communist Party's position. However, in June 1941 the Nazi invasion of Germany caused a reversal of the line of the British Communist Party, and from then until the end of the war the Communist Party came closer to entering the mainstream of British politics than it had ever done before, or has since. Women played their part in this at many levels.

Nationally the Report of the Executive Committee at the Seventeenth Party Congress held in Birmingham in 1944 recorded that a new National Women's Advisory Council had been set up, an old tenants' paper had been taken over and relaunched as a women's paper, *Woman Today*, and that the party was encouraging the setting up of special women's sections aimed to appeal particularly to housewives. In the previous year two women, Beatrix Lehmann, an actress, and Ruth Osborne, a factory worker, had been appointed to the *Daily Worker* editorial board, following a decision of the *Daily Worker* conference, that the Board must include women readers

(*Daily Worker*, 29 April, 1943).

A similar increase in women's involvement also occurred in the branches and districts. Conscription led to a shortage of men available for political activity and women moved into the district offices and took over much of the day to day work of running the party machine. Phil Piratin, the Stepney Communist Councillor who was, in 1945, to become a Communist MP, described how in London the party took steps to maintain its organization:

> Directives from the London District Committee had urged that preference should be given to women to hold leading positions, and efforts be made for their rapid development. Some women thought that this was a rather belated measure. And in view of what did happen in Stepney, I am in agreement with them ... We placed confidence in the women and they took on responsibilities which they had never been offered, or volunteered for before (Piratin, 1948).

Nor did this simply happen in London. Women took over important party jobs in other areas, perhaps most surprisingly in Fife, where a majority of party members were miners and where economic conditions and local custom had previously made it as unusual for women to take leading political roles as it was for them to work outside the home.

Communist Party women were also involved in a number of broad movements, particularly the International Women's Day committee, which revived the celebration of International Women's Day in factories and communities, and the Women's Parliaments. These were meetings of delegates from trades unions women's organizations and groups, which took place in South Wales, Lancashire, the West Riding and Scotland. The largest and most regularly organized one, though, was in London. They were (at the same time) forums for discussion on issues affecting women, like nurseries, equal pay, conditions at work and sex education, and initiators of campaigns to increase productivity and facilities for working women.

For example, in 1942-3, the London Women's Parliament organized a 'Win the War' competition. As a result of this, the Parents' Association of Buckinghamshire canvassed local women to do part-time work in the factories. Finding many unwilling to do so, because of inadequate childcare provision, the Association approached the Ministry of Health, the County Council and the local education authority to get nurseries and school meals (*Daily Worker*, 23 December, 1942). Women at the Napiers factory set up four shock brigades to increase productivity within the factory and succeeded in beating the output of skilled men. 'They take pride in the fact that they have been able to prove that there is no machine in the factory which cannot be managed by women' (*Daily Worker*, 13 January, 1943).

No doubt in all this the Communist Party's commitment to a 'total war' against fascism provided an important motivating factor. However, it would be unfair to think that the party saw women as simply factory fodder. Although there is little evidence that, in 1940, the party as a whole opposed the terms of the dilution agreement by which women were admitted to previously male jobs for the duration of the war only, in the post-war world Communists resisted attempts to restrict women's right to paid employment.

Interestingly, too, in terms of any evaluation of the party's commitment to women, as well as its undoubted commitment to the war against fascism, these struggles around women's place in paid employment were seen as not only challenging the attitude of employers to women in the workplace, but also the attitude of many male workers. Throughout the war the *Daily Worker* ran articles on women's contribution to the war effort and in this context often took issue with male prejudice. Isobel Brown, a former National Women's Organizer, for example, demanded a 'square deal for women' which, she argued, must include an improvement not only in women's wages and conditions but also 'the breaking down of the prejudice of skilled men' (*Daily Worker*, 4 February 1942). A similar approach was sometimes taken in the industrial column and by the Services Correspondent who criticised male superciliousness towards women and pointed out the range of jobs which women had taken up in the armed forces.

Communist women also fought male prejudice on the shop floor itself, as Flo Mitten, a Manchester engineer and Communist delegate, made clear in her speech to the 1941 Conference of Engineering and Allied Shop Stewards' National Council:

I represent a factory employing over three thousand women. The management in their usual way were quick to take advantage of using women for their own interests and their own betterment, but the men in the industries, surprisingly enough, stuck their heads in the sand and refused to see the possibility women had. I tackled the women and said 'Haven't you joined the Trade Unions?' They said the men didn't want them to join the unions so they never bothered. One of them had been there for thirty-two years working alongside men. She was not in the trade union because men did not ask her ... Sometimes it has been shown that women can do some jobs better and quicker than men. What are you men going to do about it? Are you going to bring up all your old prejudices? (*Shop Stewards' National Council and New Propellor*, 1941).

With women taking an increasingly important role within the party, at least at district and branch level, and possibly taking a more assertive attitude within the national leadership on women's issues even if their numerical representation at that level was still inadequate, and with the increased level of women's involvement in the trade unions, broad movements and party campaigns generally, it really did seem that 'women had stepped through the door of domesticity' (CPGB, 1944), and there was a feeling of optimism that this level of women's involvement in the public world of paid employment and politics would continue after the war. A party pamphlet, published towards the end of the war, asserted this quite clearly.

> The country's ideas have had a good shake-up. A man's job and a woman's place haven't the same meaning as before. They take an equal share of the grime and the glory, the tears and the trials, to make this world a cleaner, safer and less selfish place to live in ... (ibid.).

Keeping the Doors Open, 1945-47

In the years immediately after the war, the organization of women and women's questions continued to be important within the Communist Party. A major focus was those issues affecting women as wives and mothers, as it was in most feminist groups and in the other political parties of both the left and the right. Communist women, for example, were involved in the squatters movement, in campaigns to keep nurseries and child-welfare clinics, and in the Co-op Guild's petition against rising food prices, and in the campaign to establish the right of women to analgesia in childbirth. However, despite the closure of many factories where women had been employed, the party also fought for women's right to paid work and equal pay. That these questions were not pursued more successfully is perhaps partly due to the fact that factory branches were closed down by the Communist Party in 1945. Whilst locality-based organization probably offered more scope to women in the community, the abandoning of the very large factory branches which had been built up during the war unnecessarily limited the party's activities generally and contributed to the marginalization within the party of the problems and needs of women in the paid workforce.

Efforts were made to maintain the broad movements around women's issues. By 1945 the International Women's Day Committee was sponsored not only by the National Women's Advisory Council of the Communist Party but also by a wide range of women's groups and women's sections of other left groups. Its sponsors included ex-suffragettes, like Mrs Pethwick-Lawrence, the singer, Vera Lynn and women Members of Parliament. Its planning committee was equally broad based and included Tamara Rust, the Communist Party's National Women's Organizer, the child psychologist, Susan Isaacs, and the editors of *Woman* and *Woman's Own*. It was primarily responsible for International Women's Day celebrations. However from 1946 it also became more oriented towards campaigning, holding large meetings on Equal Pay and initiating the Peace Buses which toured the country and acted as a focus for local meetings and demonstrations.

The Cold War 1947-55

During the War, although the Government had been anxious about, and generally successful in, differentiating between support for the Soviet Union as allies and Communism as a viable system of government, the Communist Party had achieved some measure of credibility as a part of British political life. Although membership reached a peak in 1942-43 and declined from then on, apart from a small rise in 1948, this credibility was maintained to some extent in the immediate post-war years. From 1947, however, there was a build up of Cold War ideology. All cooperation with the Labour Party ceased, the BBC and Civil Service were purged, and life as a Communist could be very unpleasant indeed. As one woman in Birmingham recalled:

> We used to leaflet door to door in Birmingham. This was the old Birmingham with tenements and these had very narrow corridors and after all this had happened (the Cold War) we were very conscious about starting at the end furthest away from the stairs and working our way down. We were very conscious of escaping (Interview with author).

It is to the Communist Party's credit, therefore, that its attempts to build a broad women's movement gained impetus in this period.

In May 1949 a Communist Party Executive Committee resolution 'drew the attention of the whole Party to the special need of developing a movement among women'. It went on to single out for particular attention such issues as peace, the cost of living, social services and the position of women in industry. The following year, Tamara Rust, the Communist Party's National Women's Organiser, described women's contribution to the General Election campaign in the party's internal news and discussion journal. From her account of their activities, which included house meetings, general women's meeting and addressing the Co-op Women's Guild, she drew some interesting conclusions. Not only were these meetings 'successful and numerous only in those constituencies where our women comrades had deep roots among women neighbours', but lack of contact with women and women's organizations created a general problem for Communist women. There was, therefore, she thought, a need not only to recruit more women into the party, but also to consider the possibilities of building a broad movement of women (*World News and Views*, 15 April 1950).

Here was clearly an attempt to come to terms with the concept of women as a specific constituency whose interests could not be totally catered for by a working-class party. In order to discuss these issues a special national conference of Communist women was called in 1951. It recommended the setting up of a women's group in every branch, the appointment of a women's organizer in every branch, borough and area, and urged that the Communist Party should work with the Labour Party and the Cooperative Women's Guild in laying the basis for a broad women's movement.

Communist Party women involved in the International Women's Day Committee (IWDC) took the initiative, and in 1952 the IWDC called a National Assembly of Women to meet in London on 8 March, International Women's Day. To the delight of the organizers, fifteen hundred delegates arrived in London and an extra hall had to be hastily booked to accommodate the overflow. The delegates included representatives from trade unions, housewives' and street groups, parent-teacher associations, a dancing class and a large family in Bootle! By 1952 the National Assembly of Women's annual report was able to record a membership of five thousand, and two hundred local groups. At a NAW council meeting the following year the membership was recorded as being between seven and eight thousand organised in over three hundred and fifty groups.

Between 1951 and 1955 the Assembly was responsible for organizing national and regional International Women's Day celebrations, and for national campaigns around the Korean War, German rearmament, food prices and subsidies, and painless childbirth techniques as practised in the Soviet Union. These issues could all in some way be linked to party policy. Local groups, however, enjoyed a degree of autonomy and, in addition to supporting national campaigns, developed their own local campaigns on topics of immediate relevance to the quality of life of women in the community. They also organized social and cultural events, particularly for women and children, and recognized the politicizing effect of these kinds of activities.

The Points of Tension

This upsurge of activity created its own problems. On the one hand the party remained committed to the strategy on the 'Women Question' outlined by Lenin and Zetkin. It was particularly anxious to avoid associating itself with feminist organizations and with feminism. At the same time the practical experiences of women Communists frequently raised questions which implicitly challenged this framework.

Women in the broad movements, for example, quickly recognized that the Communist Party programme could not simply be transferred to a broad women's movement and that women had their own quite specific ideas about their needs and demands.

Madge Clifford, a member of the Bristol National Assembly of Women group, described her own experiences in *World News and Views* in 1953 and drew some lessons for the party. 'We found that women are ready to go into action,' she wrote, 'but we must have patience to listen to them and to organize around their demands. If we fail to do this then we shall find that they have moved on without us, and left us in our small sectarian circle, still talking about action' (*WNV*, 22 May 1953). In the previous year, Barbara Wiseman, another member of the NAW, and of the Surrey District Committee and the National Women's Commission, had written a basically optimistic account of the Assembly. Assessing the party's ability to go 'Forward from the Assembly', she wrote: 'The barriers between the non-Party and Party women were broken down whenever the effort was made. It is no accident that the Assembly campaign was most successful in those places where the Party had turned outwards in the past period.' Nevertheless, she recognized the dangers, for, she continued:

> At a social evening held in Surrey for some of the Assembly delegates, the most open expression of criticism came from the non-Party women in a very frank but friendly fashion. It was clear that the women, while respecting the Communists' energy and initiative, felt us to be arrogant in our attitude (*WNV*, 22 March 1952).

She went on to suggest remedies, which, while expressed with less elegance than those in *Beyond the Fragments*, carried much the same message:

> We should recognize that we talk too much and don't listen enough, consider that our methods must be right and do not draw

on the initiative of others ... are too concerned to get on with the job and not concerned enough about developing and helping people, not in a 'superior' way from above, but in a warm, human and neighbourly fashion (ibid.).

Questions of women's political activity and shared domestic responsibility were discussed with a particular immediacy in the years when the conception of the party as an elite vanguard was being challenged. Attempts at this time to restructure the party as a mass organization opened a space for the recruitment of people with different kinds and levels of commitment. This had particular implications for the involvement of housewives with domestic and childcare responsibilities. It did not mean, however, that the definition of housewives as necessarily less active than men was accepted uncritically within the party. The recruitment of housewives was merely a springboard for further debate about how to get women more involved. Domestic labour became a recurring theme both in Congress debates and in the party press.

At the Twenty-first Congress in 1949 Tamara Rust spoke of the need 'for more cooperation between men and women and a greater appreciation of women's difficulties in our own Communist families'. A letter from a woman activist in *World News and Views* took a rather terser tone: 'I agree ... that our men comrades must try to recruit their wives to the Communist Party and this should be easy where men put their oft-stated principles of equality into practice and take their full share of responsibility for home and children' (*WNV*, 26 April 1947).

In an article in the same journal in 1952 Eve Rappoport took up the question of the domestic responsibilities of Communist men at greater length and with even greater acerbity. She began by pointing to the difference between the party's ideals and the reality of life for women Communists. 'In the Communist Party,' she wrote, 'we emphasise that women have equal rights with men. But are steps taken to ensure that these rights are able to be used?' She went on to argue that, because of their domestic isolation, women needed to be involved in branch activity even more than men, and asked, 'Now, why not, comrade organizer, ask the wife along to the *Daily Worker* canvass on Sunday mornings while comrade father makes the dinner? Why not ask the mother along to the education class while father stays in to do the ironing? Why not ask the wife along to speak at meetings on Sunday night while father does the washing to save his wife a job on Monday morning, so that she can read the *Daily Worker* and the literature.'

Domestic issues were also raised in the theoretical journal *Communist Review*. Nora Jeffery, who was to become the party's National Women's Organizer, began a mainly theoretical article with a sharp piece of self-criticism:

> Rarely is there any special discussion on Party committees on how to assist women to take part in the work of the Party or the broad movements or how to overcome the special difficulties that hinder them, often because those difficulties are accepted as a natural part of a woman's life (Jeffery 1951).

Quiet Subversion

Attempts were made to give the questions raised by women out of their personal experience some political status, both in the party literature of the early fifties and, to a lesser degree, at an organizational level. Sometimes this was indirect and accidental. One woman, for example, recalled how her work on a district committee gave her access to the wives of leading male party activists and how she used this contact to help these women acquire confidence. I used to do a bit of quiet subversion, tell them they had a right to some money of their own ... maybe it did encourage some of these women to see how they could change things a bit, gave them more confidence to get involved, even if it was only in a small way' (Interview with author).

In some areas though, the need to tackle these questions was more formally recognized. In Yorkshire there were strong traditions of women in public life. Here party women's groups and NAW groups not only undertook campaigning work, but also confronted some of the personal problems faced by women, particularly those who were new to political activity. Speaking of members of a NAW group formed in Sheffield in the early fifties one woman recalled:

They were really, to be honest, wives. You know what I mean? They were wives of leading party workers in the area and of industrial comrades who joined the party because of the economic problems of the shopfloor and left their poor old wives behind. And we used to have a real old process of going to visit these women and persuading them to come to a meeting ... And from that Wortley school (a Communist school for women) was born, and that was a real occasion because there we were persuading women who had never been away from their husbands. I mean in those days. Well, nowadays, a lot of working-women go to Blackpool for the weekend, or Spain, but then a woman's place really was in the home, and to organize women to go to Wortley, it took some organization (Interview with author).

The purpose of the women's schools was not only to introduce 'women who didn't know anything about politics at all, except what their husbands fed them when they felt like it, to new ideas' (ibid.), but also to introduce them to other Communist women, and through this, to challenge their views about the relationship between femininity and political activity. 'You know, you get a situation where men go home and say to their wives, "Oh, Mary was out selling the *Daily Worker*" and those wives were thinking, "What sort of woman is she, you know, out selling the *Daily Worker*. She ought to be at home doing the cleaning" ' (ibid.).

Often such initiatives rested on the determination of individual women or groups of women. At the time of the setting up of the Wortley Women's School the Yorkshire District Organizer was Marion Ramelson, a committed supporter of women's emancipation. There was also some recognition, though, that the party as a whole should take some responsibility and challenge the relegation of some women to the role of 'party wife'. The setting up of women's sections was seen as being a step in this direction.

The Dyed-in-the-Wool Housewife

However, as the fifties progressed an increasingly mechanistic model of what socialism could offer women began to reassert itself. Whole areas of women's lives were left unquestioned. At the same time the scope of the work in the broad movements contracted. By the end of 1954 the NAW had become much more exclusively a peace movement. There were worries about declining membership and some financial problems.

Despite the contribution it had made during the war in arguing for and presenting a new definition of women's role, the *Daily Worker*, the popular face of the party within the labour movement, led the way in presenting a more restricted view of women's interests and political potential. Recipes, clothes patterns and articles on childcare, fashion and shopping, along with features on the lives of women in Eastern Europe became the standard offering in the women's section of the paper. Occasional letters complained that so many articles were directed towards the 'dyed-in-the-wool housewife' (*Daily Worker*, 5 April 1948) but to many at the time it appeared inevitable. Florence Keyworth, a journalist on the *Daily Worker* and *Morning Star* since 1945 has written: 'In the early post-war years almost half the journalists on the staff were women ... As one by one most of them left, some to start families, they were inevitably replaced by men returning from the forces. In this, as in many other ways the paper reflected developments in society at large. It all seemed very natural and fair at the time' (Keyworth, 1980).

Obviously the popular mood did play some part in defining the party's attitude towards women. During the war and in the immediate post-war years the Communist Party saw and consciously tried to mobilize 'a new spirit amongst women'. During the later forties and early fifties, though, this new spirit was increasingly defined as expressing itself most adequately in a new attitude to domestic life. Motherhood achieved a new status in the writings of John Bowlby. So too, in an economy increasingly geared to the production of consumer durables did women's role as a consumer. Moreover, it was felt that the welfare state had given working-class women the same options to enjoy this new status as middle-class women. Although married women continued to enter paid employment in greater numbers than in the past and a gradual acceptance of the right of married women to paid employment was evolving, women in this period were seen primarily as mothers and housewives. That this should find some expression in the Communist Party seems hardly surprising.

However, even during the war popular consciousness about the role of women was less advanced than is sometimes thought. Admittedly, more women were economically independent; some entered skilled trades, usually monopolized by men; and some had access to nurseries and British Restaurants.*In retrospect, however, it can be seen that these new opportunities were often undermined either by their presentation as wartime necessities, rather than women's rights, or by their containment within traditional notions of femininity.

As one recruiting poster for the Women's Services put it, 'There's an old saying, "Behind every brave man there's a woman." Yes, and she's usually a good cook. Good food is as necessary to fighting men as guns. What greater work could women do now than cook for the boys who are going to win the war for us?'

The Communist Party during the war was much less equivocal. The Home Front as understood by the Communist Party was not synonomous with the Home Front as defined by the popular press, much less with the Kitchen Front of the Ministry of Information Broadcasts and the Ministry of Food leaflets. These were devoted to advising women how to manage in the home with restricted supplies and to convincing women of the essentially patriotic nature of their domestic efforts, and their equivalence to other areas of war work. These themes were enthusiastically taken up by other government departments, like the Board of Trade with its Mrs Sew and Sew campaign, and by commercial manufacturers. In 1943 the Board of Trade was urging women to mend their families' clothes with "patriotic patches", whilst Peak Freans, the biscuit and pudding firm, were advising women as to how they could combine war work with the vital task of providing demanding husbands with a hot pudding after their evening meal. At the same time the *Daily Worker* was urging its women readers to abandon the bulk of their housework in order to contribute to the Home Front in the factories (*Daily Worker*, 13 January 1943).

Also underpinning the party's approach to women during

* Restaurants subsidized by local authorities, set up after the bombardment of London in 1940; a small number were run by voluntary helpers.

the war was the assumption that women were politically motivated and only needed gentle support and guidance. If there was any exhortation in the party press it was largely directed towards men to give women a fairer chance. The tone of the party's approach to women was very different from the hectoring one taken by the *Daily Mirror*, which assumed from the beginning of the war, through to and including the 'Vote for Him' campaign in 1945, that women were politically apathetic. At the same time the *Daily Mirror* was more anxious than the Communist press not to rupture conventional notions of femininity.

Female emancipation, according to the *Mirror*, was a good thing, but 'Let it be a quiet strength. Something restful and noble. Never should the strong side of women's nature become too obvious. Men do not want to be commanded by women; they want to be admired and adored.' The *Daily Worker*, on the other hand, regularly commended feats of heroism by British women, women in the Soviet Union and the Resistance movements which went well beyond the 'restful and noble'. In general, the feminine ideal presented to women by the *Daily Mirror* was, as befitted its Labourist politics, a fairly passive one. Writing to MPs on issues affecting their lives was seen as the peak of political involvement for most women and, although the *Mirror* did stress the number of women Labour candidates at the 1945 election, it was careful to depict them as women with traditional interests.

The slow erosion of the Communist Party's ability totally to challenge the traditional view of women's role cannot, therefore, be equated in any simple way with attitudes towards women in society at large or to the material reality of women's lives. Such factors limited the repertoire of choices open to Communist women and to the party generally, but during the war the party *had* gone beyond the consensus both in terms of the content and the style of politics which it offered to women.

Obviously a number of other factors contributed to the containment and diffusion of these efforts. Not the least important was the Communist Party's uncritical acceptance of the Soviet Union as *the* model of socialism, and the parallel belief that, within Soviet socialism, the Women Question had been solved. In addition, though, underpinning admiration for the Soviet Union and reinforced by it, was a one-dimensional vision of socialism and a belief that it could ony be achieved through a monolithic coalition of forces. The 1951 version of *The British Road to Socialism* identified forces who might be drawn together and issues which might unite them.It spoke of a 'broad popular alliance of all sections of the working people', an alliance which would include 'the industrial workers, farmers, professional people, scientists and technicians, housewives, against the handful of big landlords, bankers and monopolists who exploit them'. In no sense though, did it propose a political strategy of alliances which might unite these groups. Rather it was assumed that they could be drawn together on the basis of an already defined anti-capitalist programme and that 'such a Programme is the Programme of the Communist Party'. Specific interests and conflicting needs were not considered. The class contradiction was not merely primary, it was all-embracing. Such a framework seriously undermined the autonomy of women, not only in an immediate organizational sense, but also in the sense that it made it possible to continue to equate women's interests with class interests, and the conflicts expressed by women within the party which challenged this equation were marginalized.

Thus, the party failed to come to grips with the political problems posed by precisely those trends which facilitated the entry of more women into political activity, the combined strategies of a broad front and a mass movement. Instead, it opted slowly and not without considerable tensions and opposition on the way, for the view that these strategies could be based on existing working-class culture and aspirations. Thus, the political transformation of this culture, which might have taken account of the interests of different constituencies within the mass movement, never took place.

Communist women, through their political activity and demands for shared domestic responsibility, had repeatedly challenged one aspect of working-class culture: namely the sexual division of labour. Instead of opening the way to further changes, this challenge was contained. Its defeat in the mid-fifties can be summed up in one woman's description of a friend, who was a prominent Communist:

> She used to say to me: 'Never let it be said that she does a grand job for the working-class movement, but she doesn't wash her windows.' These are working-class values, you see (Interview with author).

Thanks to Jon Bloomfield, Ruth and Eddie Frow, Connie Seifert and not the least, to Rosalind Brunt and Caroline Rowan whose contribution to this article has gone beyond that expected of editors. I also owe a special debt to all the women who have talked to me about their experience in the Communist Party in the forties and fifties. Even when sometimes disagreeing with my analysis they have been unfailingly generous and supportive.

References

Carrillo, Santiago (1977), *Eurocommunism and the State*, London, Lawrence and Wishart.

Communist Party of Great Britain (1944), *A Women's Place*, London, CPGB.

Daily Worker, September 1942-1955 (The *Daily Worker* was banned from January 1941 to September 1942).

Delmar, Rosalind (1976), 'Looking again at Engels's *Origin of the Family, Private Property and the State*', in Oakley A., and Mitchell J. (eds), *The Rights and Wrongs of Women*, Harmondsworth, Penguin.

Jeffery, Nora (1951) 'Women in Class Society', *Communist Review*, April.

Keyworth, Florence (1980), 'Women and the *Daily Worker*' *Link*, Communist Party Women's Journal, Summer.

Lenin, V.I. and Zetkin, K., *On the Emancipation of Women*, Moscow: Progress Publishers. I have been unable to find much of Zetkin's writing in translation although there are a number of left groups who have published extracts (e.g. *International Socialism* (First series), No 44 contains edited extracts of her speech to the Fourth Congress of the Communist International in which she outlined some of the principles discussed here.) However, *On the Emancipation of Women*, although ascribed entirely to Lenin by the publishers contains as an appendix, a long extract from Zetkin's *Recollections of Lenin*.

Piratin, Phil (1948), *Our Flag Stays Red*, London, Thames Publications (reprinted by Lawrence and Wishart, 1978).

Rowbotham, Sheila (1972), *Women, Resistance and Revolution* Harmondsworth, Penguin.

Rowbotham, S., Segal, L., Wainwright, H. (1979), *Beyond the Fragments: Feminism and the Making of Socialism*, Newcastle Socialist Centre and Islington Community Press, London.

Sacks, Karen (1974) 'Engels revisited; Women, the Organisation of Production and Private Property', in Rosaldo and Lamphere (eds), *Women, Culture and Society*, Stanford, California, Stanford University Press.

Shop Stewards' National Council and New Propellor (1941), *Arms and the Men: Report of the Conference of the Engineering and Allied Trades*, London (despite its title the cover of this publication shows a woman worker, graphically illustrating the contradictions within women's position in the paid work-force during the Second World War).

Taylor, Barbara (1979), 'The Men are as Bad as their Masters: Socialism, Feminism and Sexual Antagonism in the London Tailoring Trade in the early 1930s', in *Feminist Studies*, University of Maryland, Spring.

Taylor, Barbara (1981), 'Socialist Feminism: Utopian or Scientific', in Samuel (ed), *People's History and Socialist Theory*, London, Routledge and Kegan Paul.

World News and Views, 1943-55.

The Family In Socialist-Feminist Politics

Mary McIntosh

A central task of socialist-feminist theory must be to explore the relations of the existing form of women's oppression to the existing form of capitalism. We need to try to guage how much we can achieve towards women's liberation under capitalism and also what obstacles will still remain in socialist society. It is important, then, to develop an understanding of the family, as the core institution of the oppression of women. How does the ideal of the family affect women's and men's actual lives? How does it relate to the capitalist system of production? How does it perpetuate existing models of masculinity and femininity? How does it enable men to oppress women? A good deal has been written on these subjects, some of it at a highly abstract level, some rich in historical detail, some schematic and over-simplified.

Drawing on this material, this paper will set out some of the major recent critiques of the family, first those from a socialist perspective, then those from a feminist one. Feminists have sometimes been disheartened by those non-feminist approaches that appear to suggest that since the family is a vital pillar in the capitalist edifice it cannot be modified under capitalism. The logic of this argument will be unpicked and it will be shown that it is possible to trace a supportive relation between the institution of the family and capitalism without being reduced to a pessimistic determinism about the possibilities for change. Current socialist politics can therefore begin to develop strategies based on the socialist-feminist critique of the family, and some of these will be outlined at the end of this paper (section IV). But before these can be developed some account must be given of how the idea of family life has great attractiveness for many people in contemporary society (section III). This does not detract from the overall critique of the family, but it must be taken seriously in any thinking about how to implement that critique.

I. Critiques of the family: socialist and feminist

The critique of the bourgeois family had long been a part of socialist thought; but the new feminism of the 1970s stimulated its revival. Some of the major contributions to Marxist theory during this period were in the elaboration of the ways in which the family system helps to create and reproduce the conditions necessary for capitalist production. The best-known discussions in this area have been called the 'domestic labour debate' (see, for instance Seccombe, 1974; Molyneux, 1979; Malos, 1980). It has been common in socialist and feminist thought to see housework as degrading and repetitive drudgery which lacked the elements of creativity and social participation embodied in work in even the most mechanized factory. With the beginnings of the women's liberation movement came a new perception of housework – as a form of production. In 1969 Margaret Benston identified it as a pre-capitalist, indeed pre-commodity, form of production, the production of use-values, goods and services for direct consumption in the family rather than for sale. Later writers went further and saw housework not simply as a different, archaic, form of production existing alongside capitalist production, but as the production and reproduction of a commodity essential to capitalism, namely labour power itself. The 'debate' had a number of dimensions to it: whether housework was 'productive' or 'unproductive' in the technical Marxist sense of producing surplus value, whether housework was an integral part of the capitalist mode of production or had only an indirect relation to it, whether unpaid housework served to raise or lower the value of the husband's labour power, whether or not housewives were part of the working class, whether what is now done as housework could ever be socialized under capitalism. But there was an underlying acceptance of a view that was quite new to Marxist thought, that housework was important and that it played an economic part in the reproduction of capitalism.

For some, the question of the position of the housewife was the same as the question of the position of women, since all women were destined to unpaid labour in the home as a primary role. Others pointed out that 'the central feature of women's oppression under capitalism is the fact that they are *both* domestic and wage labourers' (Coulson *et al.*, 1975). Yet all agreed that housework, rather than consumption, was the key to the economic relation between the family and capitalist production.

In this context, other aspects of the relation were seen as relatively minor, though tending to work in the same direction, with the family functioning to reproduce the conditions for capitalism. The contribution of the privatized household and privatized leisure to raising levels of demand for consumer goods was seen as helping to combat the tendency to over-production. The partial economic dependence of wives on their husbands was seen as enabling capital to treat married women as a 'reserve army of labour' to be mobilized and demobilized according to the need for labour in capitalist production (Milkman, 1976; Humphries, 1976; Beechey, 1977; Bruegel, 1979). Some groups of male workers have been helped to secure higher wages by the idea of the 'family wage': the idea that men need to earn wages sufficient to support a wife and children. But these have been a privileged section of craft workers and on the whole the idea of the family wage has helped to divide and weaken the working class, dividing men who could support their wives from those who could not and dividing men from women (Barrett and McIntosh, 1980).

Finally, following Louis Althusser (1971), the family was seen as an 'Ideological State Apparatus', serving to provide not only for the material reproduction of labour power but also for the reproduction of skills and of 'submission to the rules of the established order' (Althusser, 1971: 127). The family turns out little replicas of the parents, people suited to life in bourgeois society: individualistic yet subservient, acquisitive, calculative, socially rootless. And family responsibilities oblige adults to go out to work regularly in order to house and support their families.

This new socialist analysis – the perception of the existing family, with unpaid domestic work by women as its key characteristic, as a necessary or at least very important prop to the capitalist system – was matched by a feminist analysis of the family as the primary location of women's specific oppression as women. Feminist developments of the psychoanalytic tradition emphasized the part played by the asymmetry between parents in the production of femininity and masculinity in their girl and boy children (Mitchell, 1974; Chodorow, 1978). The first attachment, for both girls and boys, is to a woman who 'mothers' them; the relation to the father is later and less close. So from the start, the individual develops in relation to a woman and a man who are clearly distinct. The complex processes are variously theorized by different schools of psychoanalytic thought, but all would agree that in general the result is a reproduction in the offspring of the femininity and masculinity of the parents.

Some feminists have concluded from this that femininity, characterized according to Juliet Mitchell by narcissism, masochism and passivity, is too deeply engrained to be readily removed. Many of those who have maintained an interest in psychoanalytic theory have either been concerned with feminist therapy or else, like many contributors to the magazine *m/f*, have abandoned the attempt to specify a programme for change (see, for instance, Coward *et al.*, 1976). Others, like Gayle Rubin (1975) and Nancy Chodorow (1978), have argued that it shows how important it is to challenge women's exclusive responsibility for early childcare and to break the division of labour among parents in order to produce a new generation in which the polarization between feminine and masculine is less marked.

A quite different feminist critique of the family sees housework and other domestic responsibilities as the focal point of women's oppression. Christine Delphy (1976) put it graphically by describing marriage as a 'work contact' by which the head of the family appropriates all the work done in the family, especially, nowadays, his wife's work in providing domestic services and raising children. Delphy (1977: 15) even went so far as to describe marriage as a 'relationship of slavery'. Lenin (1920) had also written of the importance of freeing women from "domestic slavery", to free them from their stupefying and humiliating subjugation to the eternal drudgery of the kitchen and the kitchen and the nursery'. The proponents of 'wages for housework' have also stressed the unpaid nature of domestic work as being its chief disadvantage, though they emphasize its contribution to capitalist production rather than to the ease and comfort of men's lives, as Delphy would (see Dalla Costa and James, 1972).

Others, often outside the Marxist tradition altogether, have explored the consequences for the rest of women's lives. Women's responsibility for household chores and for caring for children and others at home has a profound and far-reaching effect on every other aspect of their lives. On the one hand, it creates great problems for them in taking paid work outside the home. The phenomenon known to sociology by the banal phrases 'women's two roles', or 'the double shift', is a painful reality in most women's lives. But recent analysis, and particularly historical work, has deepened our understanding of it and brought us to see that men are involved too; that it is a relation between the division of labour in the home and the division of labour in paid work; that men's lack of responsibility for household cares and the service they get from their wives enable them to work longer hours, to continue going out to work through family crises, to travel further to get better jobs, to undertake training and pursue careers.

On the other hand, along with the wife's responsibilities goes the assumption of the husband's duty to maintain his family: the idea of the breadwinner and the dependent wife. On this basis men have successfully claimed the better-paid jobs for themselves and claimed higher pay even when doing the same jobs as women.

The question of the 'family wage' has recently been debated amongst feminists (Humphries, 1977; Barrett and McIntosh, 1980; Land, 1980). In the nineteenth century, there were many who considered it a great advance that men should be able to support a wife and children on their own wage and that women could stay at home and devote themselves to the care of the family. Some feminists opposed this, on egalitarian grounds, but others accused them of being out of touch with the harsh realities of working-class life if they thought that the opportunity to work in a factory brought benefits comparable to work in a profession. But now that infancy takes up such a brief period of parents' lives and that feminists have adopted the goal of socializing domestic work and childcare (as well as the hours in factories being shorter and the work less strenuous), the assumption that a husband should support his wife has been firmly rejected by feminists. The increasing number of married women going out to paid work and the incompatibility between the ideas of 'equal pay' and 'the family wage' have strengthened this rejection.

Furthermore, although it is true that women are responsible for housework, it is not true that they can rely on being supported by a breadwinner. Yet social security, income tax and ideas embedded in education and job selection and training all assume that they can (Land, 1976, 1978). The fifth demand of the British Women's Liberation Movement, the demand for legal and financial independence, has focussed campaigns around these issues and constantly emphasized that dependence has psychological as well as economic disadvantages (Gieve *et al.*, 1974). Lack of autonomy, degradation, the need to manipulate personal relations, tend to stunt women's potential and make them insecure and unadventurous. Indeed, it could be argued that some of the undesirable features of 'femininity', which Juliet Mitchell and others in the psychoanalytic tradition have explained in terms of the experiences of infancy, can equally be explained by the adult situation of dependence and the practical need to seek material support.

The feminist critique of the family as the tap-root of the specific oppression of women is not, of course, new. It had long been a theme of feminist thought. Olive Schreiner, for instance, had devoted the first half of her book *Woman and Labour*, published in 1911, to what she luridly named women's 'parasitism' within marriage. But socialist feminists of the 1970s were tempted to put this critique to a new use. They linked it with the new socialist critique of the family (which was itself largely developed by women, or in relation to the Women's Liberation Movement). So there developed the view

that socialism and feminism are united in their opposition to
the family, as a prop of capitalism and as a source of women's
oppression.

II. Functions and interests

The simple formula that 'the family is a prop to capitalism',
though true enough, is not in itself adequate for a political
analysis. Indeed the ultimate convergence of feminism and
socialism in a rejection of the family has often been used to
argue for the postponement of feminist politics until the
achievement of socialism. Much to the chagrin of socialist
feminists, some socialists have argued that because the family is
functional to the capitalist system, in the sense that it helps to
keep it going, it is fundamentally capitalist, rather than, say,
patriarchal, in character, and cannot be transformed under
capitalism. Many feminists have retorted that this functionalist
argument is a form of rigid economic determinism and so have
rejected any attempt to specify functional relations between
family and capitalism. This polarization is, I believe, a false
one. The confusions underlying it have their roots in a more
general debate about 'Marxist functionalism'.

'Marxist functionalism' has been much criticized in Britain
recently, largely because it has become tarred with the same
brush as economic reductionism – the misreading of
materialism that sees everything as a mere effect of economic
forces. Just as the reaction against Stalinism has catapulted
some people away from socialism altogether, so the reaction
against home-made imitations of Althusser's theories often
takes the form of a rejection of any kind of functional analysis,
and sometimes of any kind of Marxism at all. A number of
arguments, some acceptable and some unacceptable, seem to
be wrapped up in this rejection. In many ways they echo the
arguments that took place in the late 1950s within American
sociology. For 'Marxist funcionalism' at first sight appears to
be very much akin to sociological functionalism in its logical
structure.

Sociological functionalism (and anthropological
functionalism is very similar) rejects the study of the causes of
social phenomena in favour of a study of their functional

interrelations. Arguing that any society that endures must be in some way integrated into a whole, with a set of institutions that tend overall to contribute to its survival rather than to its disintegration, it sets out to study the various ways in which institutions function for the maintenance of the whole social system. 'Marxist functionalism' is similar, being based on Althusser's dictum that 'every child knows that a social formation which did not reproduce the conditions of production at the same time as it produced would not last a year' (Althusser, 1971: 123).*

The first difference is that instead of a concern with a decentred 'social system' in which a set of social institutions all play equal and complementary parts, Marxist analysis is concerned with the reproduction of a specific mode of production. Production, and the forces and relations of production, are at the centre of the stage, though there is dispute as to how to describe their relation to the rest of the social formation. The second difference is that there can be no 'Marxist functionalism' as a total theory of society, bypassing causal analysis, bypassing dialectical materialism. In Marxism, there can only be functional analysis, which traces the ways in which various social phenomena contribute to the reproduction of the mode of production. To trace these functions is not to discover the causes of the phenomena in question, nor to say that they are determined by the mode of production. Its aim is to specify the requirements for the reproduction of capitalism and to ask whether and how that reproduction is accomplished. It does not provide a complete model of society, but offers a way of exploring some relationships between social institutions.

Sociological functionalism was criticized in the 1950s for being teleological (that is, for explaining things in terms of their supposed purposes, or the functions they fulfil). It was criticized for being static, in the sense that it saw each element of society as necessary to the whole and therefore

---

* Althusser appears to attribute this statement to Marx, in a letter to Kugelmann, 11 July 1868, *Selected Correspondence*, Moscow 1955, p. 209. But as the statement does not appear in that letter, at least in the English translation, and as in any case it was Althusser who introduced the idea to British readers, it seems safer to refer to it as 'Althusser's dictum'.

unchangeable. It was criticized for being conservative, since any change would upset social equilibrium and so must be condemned. And it was criticized for concentrating on structure rather than on people as social agents and so being anti-humanist and unable to understand social conflict and power. Against all but the last criticism it was able to defend itself by defining and recognizing its own limitations. Its most systematic apologist, Robert K. Merton (1957), even introduced the term 'dysfunction' to indicate that institutions could in some respects tend to disrupt as well as preserve social integration.

Marxist functionalist analysis has never needed to trim its sails quite this way since it has never claimed to be more than a phase in a wider analysis, usually a class analysis. Thus when people have studied, say, education as an ideological state apparatus, they have not stopped there but have gone on to explore how education also undermines certain interests of the ruling class, how educational institutions develop their own autonomous logic which may limit their usefulness as a tool for capitalist reproduction, how struggles between classes and class fragments, between national groups and other sections, have also affected the character of the educational system.

The purpose of functional analysis should simply be to work out what the long-term interests of the ruling class will be, since these will be the dominant factor affecting the policies of the state and many other institutions. So it is not true to say, as Jill Hodges and Athar Hussain (1979) do, that 'the approach starts with the presumption that the conditions of existence of relations and institutions are ultimately the functions which they themselves perform in the reproduction of the social relations of production' (pp 89-90). For functional analysis is quite distinct from causal analysis. Hodges and Hussain mistake the argument of most writers who have explored the functions of the family when they say it is that:

> the family under capitalism exists because it performs an essential role in the reproduction of the relations of production, namely the reproduction of labour power ... There is ... a wide variety of Marxist functionalist analyses ... but ... All of them transform the question 'why does the family exist?' into 'what function does the

idealized family perform in the reproduction of the social relations of production of capitalism?'

The same conflation of functional analysis with causal analysis is made by Paul Hirst: 'Theories of ... modern family forms as necessary to capitalist reproduction attempt to place [this question] within the confines of a conventional socialist analysis, to subordinate them to a causality governed by the economic' (1979: 13).

Such criticisms apply only to those who are foolish enough to embrace functionalism as an explanatory model – the only example I can think of is the Revolutionary Communist Group's 1976 article, though even there the capitalist class enters as an agent, so it is not a purely structural interpretation. Hodges and Hussain's criticism is not relevant, as they imply, to all analysis of the functions that institutions play for the reproduction of the mode of production.

The purpose of their criticism, however, is not to propose a more adequate or elaborated Marxist analysis but to present an interpretation of the work of Jacques Donzelot who, they claim, sees the family as 'the point of intersection of different social practices: medical, judicial, educational, psychiatric, etc.' and, although he describes a 'strategy' towards the family, does not see this strategy as emanating from any particular social group. They are thus throwing the baby out with the bathwater. Their real purpose is to reject Marxism, but they cast this in terms of a critique of an ossified Marxist functionalism. So eager are they to reject an approach they see as tending to class reductionism, that they turn to one that gives no primacy to production or to class and class struggle in its understanding of social phenomena.

One reason why this debate has generated such a lot of heat is that it is thought to have a direct relation to political strategy. So, for instance, for Paul Hirst the rejection of functional arguments leads to the view that women's struggle is one that 'cannot be aligned in terms of capitalism and anti-capitalism', whereas for the Revolutionary Communist Group their functionalist analysis leads them to believe that 'it is capital itself that perpetuates the conditions of women's inequality and that 'there is no separation between the interests of women and the independent interests of the working class as a whole. Both interests can only be defended by overthrowing capitalism' (1976: 47).

If such a political polarization has its roots in the acceptance or rejection of functional analysis, then a Hirst must believe that no sectional struggles other than those of the pure proletariat and the pure capitalist class can be aligned in terms of capitalism and anti-capitalism and the RCG must believe that all sectional struggles can be so aligned. In fact, of course, there are many steps between the general stance on functionalism and the political application in any particular case. My contention is that some of these steps involve the study of the functions that social practices oppressive of women serve for capitalism. In the end, though, in my view, women's struggle can neither be subsumed under anti-capitalism nor divorced from it, but the character of each must be profoundly influenced by the other.

So the line of criticism of functionalism that confuses it with economic reductionism is neither apposite nor fruitful. However, there are more common mistakes in the interpretation of functional analysis that are worth pointing to. One is a political one: the assumption that if we can show something is functional for maintaining capitalism and thus in the interests of the capitalist class it must necessarily be against the interest of the working class.

It is, of course, true that the central interests of the two classes are antagonistic and in particular that the wage relation is an antagonistic one. The capitalist interest lies in lowering wages, the proletarian in raising them. In the long-term the proletarian interest lies in abolishing the wage-relation altogether, whereas the existence of the capitalist depends upon its survival. But within capitalism, we get a very different picture if we look at the other face of the wage, as the means of feeding and clothing the workers. For the satisfaction of the worker's basic needs is in the interests of both capitalists (who want their labour power reproduced) and of workers, who want food and clothes. Where they may differ is about what food and clothes, what other needs should be met and under what conditions.

So the question of the politics of the family, which is after all from this perspective part of the means by which proletarian needs are met, cannot be resolved simply by the discovery that some features of it serve the interests of the capitalist class. For this would not of itself preclude them serving proletarian interests as well.

From a political perspective, then, it is not so important that unpaid domestic labour reduces the value of labour power overall (thereby benefitting capital) as that it reduces the level of wages overall by dividing workers into breadwinners and semi-dependants and enabling women to be used as an industrial reserve army (see Barrett and McIntosh, 1980).

However, the point of view of the working class as a whole is not, in general, the point of view of individual members of the working class. It is not even the point of view articulated in trade-union consciousness. But it is, or should be, the point of view adopted by socialists. The socialist critique of the ideal of the working-class family in capitalist society – the family of the bread-winning husband and the houseworking wife – is that it is divisive of the working class. This means that it divides men against women by benefitting men at the expense of women. So men, in order to preserve a modicum of privilege within their underprivileged situation have an interest in the short term in maintaining the existing idea of the family.

Another common mistake in functional analysis is the assumption that every institution that exists has a positive function to perform and that once that has been identified the matter rests. In fact, however, any institution may function in a number of different ways and these may well be contradictory. Thus, for instance, I have argued (1978) that the existing family household system functions both to provide for the cheap reproduction of labour power and also to maintain married women as a reserve army of labour. At some periods these two functions may go hand in hand; at others there may be a severe contradiction between the need to mobilize women into the capitalist labour force and the need to keep them busy at their household duties. An interesting feature of the contemporary family is its flexibility: it survives through these alternating periods and family motivation is sufficiently strong to make women do enormous amounts of unpaid domestic labour even when they are going out to work as well. As Irene Bruegel (1978: 12) has put it: 'We are dealing with tendencies, which resolve themselves in contradictory ways, rather than with one-dimensional functions.'

Finally, another common error in interpreting functional analysis is the idea of functional necessity. Sociological functionalism was accused of being conservative because it was thought to claim that 'what is must be' since, having shown how an institution functioned to preserve the whole, it had demonstrated that it was a necessary element of society. Against this, Merton argued that there could be 'functional alternatives', that one institution could be replaced by others without the whole edifice collapsing. No particular institution was indispensable; functional analysis merely pointed out that certain functions would need to be fulfilled somehow. The inverse accusation has been made against 'Marxist functionalism' – that it leads to the conclusion that nothing can change within capitalism and that all improvements must await the great revolutionary catastrophe. It is true that some writers have reached this conclusion (Revolutionary Communist Group, 1976, and Smith, 1978), arguing that since privatized domestic labour is functional for capital the form of the family cannot be altered under capitalism. Such arguments need to be unpicked. 'Privatized domestic labour' is not the same as 'the form of the family'; as Irene Bruegel (1978: 4) has pointed out, we need to take into account male domination and sex-role differentiation as well. So it might be possible under capitalism to have a new form of the family with private but equally shared domestic labour. Or, better, it might be possible to think of (and therefore campaign for) new ways of reproducing labour power under capitalism. Some writers have claimed that this is in principle incompatible with the reproduction of the *free* wage labourers necessary for the capitalist wage relation (Himmelweit and Mohun, 1977; Smith, 1978; Seccombe, 1980). My view, on the other hand, is that there could be functional alternatives to private domestic labour which did not necessarily involve a single agency (let alone 'capital') taking over the whole responsibility for all aspects of the reproduction of labourers and which did not therefore involve the ownership of the labourers by anyone but themselves.

   The question of whether or how such functional alternatives are likely to emerge to replace the existing family form is another matter altogether, and depends in part upon the demands that are made by the Women's Movement and whether these are taken up by the working class and its allies. 'Capitalism both tends to destroy the family and to maintain it' (Bruegel, 1978: 12). Capitalism has a tendency to extend the sphere of commodity production and this has affected domestic production. The baking and brewing, sewing and laundering, scrubbing of floors and fetching of coals that made up housework in the nineteenth century have all been replaced or modified by commodities. Social workers, doctors, teachers, the courts, all intervene in family life, regulating relations between husband and wife, parents and children. How much further will such tendencies develop and will new alternatives for family functions emerge?

III. The Appeal of the Family

One reason why the future of the family may appear to be in the hands of the capitalists or subject to the inexorable 'logic of capitalism' is that we have not developed a politics in this area. Only a tiny fraction of the working class, and even of active socialists, accept the need to transform the family, though it has been a part of socialist and Marxist thinking for long enough. An even tinier fraction of women would see the family as the root of their oppression, though the Women's Liberation Movement is beginning to make some changes here. Unless we are to ascribe this to simple 'false consciousness', calling for a barrage of radical propoganda to bring people in touch with reality, it must mean that the question is rather more complex.

   To understand this we need to take quite seriously the arguments in defence of the family that have been put forward by many socialists and by people otherwise sympathetic to feminism. It is important to distinguish those who defend the form of the family existing (or thought to exist) in capitalis societies from those who, like Frederick Engels (1968) have envisaged an ideal socialist family, heterosexual and monogamous, but based on equality and love, not on male dominance and indissolubility. Engels could entertain that idea because he believed that male dominance in the family was associated with private property and thus had a material basis in the bourgeois family which it did not have in the family of the propertyless proletariat and would not have in any socialist society. Recent theory, however, has had to recognize that working-class male dominance is not merely a left-over from pre-capitalist days but has developed new roots among the waged and salaried workers in capitalist (and indeed in socialist) societies. We have come to see the private rearing of children in the heterosexual, monogamous nuclear-family-household as inseparable from male dominance, so that we cannot imagine jettisoning the bad bits and preserving the good bits, as Engels could.

It is important, too, to distinguish those who justify the family as natural or inevitable, not questioning the historical variability of its forms, and those who see the family (and especially the working-class family) as an appropriate economic, cultural and emotional form in capitalist society. Socialists usually see capitalism as a distinct epoch with specific social forms; nevertheless, they do not always wish to condemn all of these forms but see many of them as products of proletarian struggle, whether defensive bastions or embryonic socialist forms. So, many would accept the view of Christopher Lasch (1977) of the family as a 'haven in a heartless world', and many would accept the view of Jane Humphries (1977) that, given the material conditions of the working class, the family and kinship networks provide a valuable defensive system. They provide, according to her, for mutual support free from state interference; they help support women and children outside the labour market and so improve male workers' bargaining power; and they play a role in developing class consciousness and class struggle.

In considering these justifications, it is helpful to introduce the notion of *secondary gains*. Secondary gains are advantages that people are able to establish in a situation whose primary character is disadvantageous. So, for instance a farm labourer may be very badly paid, but have a tied cottage at low rent and access to many 'perks' provided he is deferential to the farmer and his family. Or a harem-dweller may lack freedom but live in great comfort and security, having every need met without effort or care. The problem with such secondary gains is that they may become so important to people that they do everything they can to defend them and do not try to alter the primary oppression. The farm labourer may be afraid to join the union that might get his pay raised, for fear of angering the farmer and losing his cottage or his 'perks'. The concubine may come to rely on others to look after her and not even consider escape or revolt, let alone anything that might change the harem system.

To some extent, this is so with the family: it does offer some compensation for the rigours of working-class life. People often prefer home to work or school, home cooking to canteen food, their 'nearest and dearest' to the ever-changing contacts at work and in the streets. Often they love to be 'out', at work or at leisure, and men who retire or lose their jobs feel trapped and bored at home. But they want the home to be there behind them. 'Home is the place where when you have to go there they have to let you in,' as Ogden Nash once put it. The home offers us security, protectiveness, dependence, intimacy, support, as well as more practical advantages. Its emotional and psychological appeal is immense.

But the family and its context are dialectically related: just as 'monogamy' depends upon prostitution, so prostitution depends upon 'monogamy'. In the same way, the quality of work and school life, the quality of canteen food, the quality of relationships at work and in the streets are all premissed on the idea that everyone has a satisfying home to go back to. Yet, apart from the fact that many people do not have homes at all, there is much to suggest that many homes are far from satisfactory to their members and may have a bad effect on some of them. For example, whereas single men are more likely than married men to be treated for mental illness, the reverse is the case for women. The family as a refuge is probably a wishful idea rather than a reality. It is an idea that is fostered by the mass media – think of all those cosy advertisements for drinking chocolate and central heating –

and by schools, religion and social workers.

Writing of the life-cycle of the family, Lee Comer (1973) said:

> If we see the whole cycle as a film with a beginning, a middle and an end, we can see that the time when parents and children are living together has been caught in a static frame and blown up out of all proportion and is so projected as to signify the rest of the film. So it is that the family unit is the peak of the pyramid of the social hierarchy against which individual lives appear as one long 'before and after'.

Less than one-third of the country's households consist of a man, a woman and their dependent children and most people spend less than half of their lives in an intact family unit. So the image conjured up by the politicians and moralists – not to mention housing officers – when they defend 'the family' is an image of a minority presented as if it were the overwhelming majority. Yet it is an immensely powerful image for all of us. 'The dream of happy families,' as Lee Comer puts it, 'is a static dream to cherish which is never quite fantasy because it's always round the corner or somebody else has it.'

The secondary gains that the family offers are thus for many people illusory, or at best short-lived. Yet the illusion is a powerful one because it is based on a reality – even if on a reality that is unattainable for many. For, given the existence of – or at least the belief in – the family system, people usually are better off materially in families than they would be outside them. This is especially true of women, who cannot earn such good wages and who often have the impediment of having to care for children or for old and disabled people. Since state support is either non-existent or inadequate, they may feel safer if they have a husband to support them, despite the fact that husbands too are frequently unable or unwilling to give adequate support and that the condition of such support is subordination. As Diane Elson and Ruth Pearson (1981) put it, writing of women in the Third World:

> It may seem paradoxical to talk of the protection afforded by subordination, but the paradox lies in the social relations themselves. When the social identity of women has to be established through their relations with men, the absence of father, brother or husband is often disadvantageous.

But if we ask *why* women's social identity has to be established through men, or in Britain, *why* women's wages are lower than men's, *why* women more often have to care for children and others, *why* state support is not good enough, we can see that though families may appear to offer secondary gains to individual women, the family as a system is the very reason for their primary oppression.

IV. Strategies for Change

Both socialist and feminist critiques of the family need to be enriched by an understanding of the secondary gains, both real and spurious, that the family offers. We cannot make the immediate abolition of the family our sole demand. What is needed is a strategy to transform it by providing alternatives to the secondary gains it offers.

An example is the strategy adopted by the Women's Liberation Movement – and indeed by some earlier feminists. This is the strategy of seeking to establish ways in which women can survive without dependence upon a husband. In a sense, four out of the first seven demands made by the British Women's Liberation Movement were directed to this goal: Equal Pay, Equal Educational and Job Opportunities. Twenty-four-hour Nurseries, Financial and Legal Independence. Even the demands about contraception and abortion, sexuality and freedom from male violence have a dimension that relates to building possibilities for independence from men. As these develop, so the *need* for a dependent marriage as a compensation will decline and women will be able to enter marriages, or not enter them, on their own terms.

So the strategy is not to say: 'a husband's social security, or his pension, or his pay, should not include an element for his wife because she should not be dependent', but to say: 'a married woman should have a right to pay or benefit adequate to her support, in her own right'. It is not to say 'people should not get married', but to say: 'people should not feel they have to get married in order to survive emotionally and materially'.

Similarly, we need to build a welfare state as a non-family

system for mutual support and care, and to strive for working-class control and localized control so that it can really meet people's needs. At present, state institutions like nurseries, children's homes, hospitals, mental hospitals, special homes, accomodation for the 'homeless', old people's homes, are all vastly inferior in most ways – from facilities to 'atmosphere' – to what the average family could offer. So we tend to think of state provision as being necessarily inferior to family provision. But this is largely because it is in short supply, under-funded, bureaucratically organized and is commonly regarded as a substitute for the 'real thing', which is family care (or rather, care by a female relative).

The experience of education shows us that when state provision is properly funded and undertaken purposively, rather than as a safety net, it can be much better, more stimulating and more truly social than anything a family could provide. This could be true for the care of the old, ill and disabled as well. The image of being 'put away' is justified at present, but only because institutions are cut off from the local community, unknown, forbidding and impersonal. We must create visions, and if possible examples, of socially provided care that is better than family care because it is available to all, even those without relatives, and because it does not force people into dependence and unwanted interference from their children or others who look after them.

We must also develop a socialist and feminist culture in which the ideology of the family is constantly questioned. For instance, there should continue to be pressure to provide crêches so that parents of young children can attend meetings and conferences. But we should by now be beginning to recognize that we want this to be a short-term need. The demand for a crêche merely highlights the wider problems of parents. For the long term there should be more stable local alternatives to individual parental care. The neighbourhood nursery where the child is known and which is part of her daily life should have responsibility, and indeed rights, in relation to every child, and private parenting should become less and less the privileged and total form of childcare. At present such ideas are utopian, but unless they are discussed and kept alive in the context of today's more primitive struggles we shall have only a partial socialism and a token feminism.

Since this article was written, Michèle Barrett and I have dealt at greater length with the analytical and political questions raised here (The Anti-Social Family, *London:* Verso, 1982).

References

Allen, Sandra *et al.,* (editors), *Conditions of Illusion,* Leeds: Feminist Books, (1974).

Althusser, Louis, 'Ideology and Ideological State Apparatuses', in *Lenin and Philosophy and other essays,* New Left Books, (1971)

Barker, D.L. and Allen, S. (editors), *Sexual Divisions and Society: Process and Change,* London, Tavistock (1976).

Barrett, Michèle and McIntosh, Mary, 'The "Family Wage": Some Problems for Socialists and Feminists', *Capital and Class,* No. 11, pp. 51-72 (1980).

Beechey, Veronica 'Some Notes on Female Wage Labour in Capitalist Production', *Capital and Class,* No. 3 (1977).

Bruegel, Irene 'Women as a Reserve Army of Labour', *Feminist Review,* No. 3 (September 1979).

Chodorow, Nancy, *The Reproduction of Mothering: Psychoanalysis and the Sociology of Gender,* Berkeley: University of California Press, (1978).

Comer, Lee, 'Functions of the Family', *Red Rag,* 1973, reprinted in Allen, 1974.

Coulson, Margaret, Magas, Branka and Wainwright, Hilary 'The Housewife and Her Labour under Capitalism – a critique', *New Left Review,* No. 89 (January-February 1975) – reprinted in Malos, 1980.

Coward, Rosalind, Lipshitz, Sue and Cowie, Elizabeth, 'Psychoanalysis and Patriarchal Structures', in Women's Publishing Collective (1976)

Dalla Costa, Maria rosa and James, Selma, *The Power of Women and the Subversion of the Community,* a 1972 pamphlet reprinted in Malos, (1980)

Delphy, Christine, 'Continuous and Disontinuities in Marriage and Divorce' in Barker and Allen (eds) (1976).

Delphy, Christine, 'The Main Enemy' in *The Main Enemy: A Materialis Analysis of Women's Oppression,* London, Women's Research and Resources Centre, (1977).

Elson, Diane and Pearson, Ruth, 'Nimble Fingers Make Cheap Workers *Feminist Review,* No. 7 (1981).

Engels, Frederick, 'The Origin of the Family, Private Property and the State' in *Marx and Engels: Selected Works in One Volume* London: Lawrence & Wishart (1968).

Fox, Bonnie (editor), *Hidden in the Household,* Toronto: The Women's Press 1980.

Gieve, Katherine et al., 'The Independence Demand' in Sandra Allen *et. al.* (editors) (1974).

Himmelweit, Susan and Mohun, Simon 'Domestic Labour and Capital', *Cambridge Journal of Economics*, No. 1 (1977).

Hirst, Paul *On Law and Ideology*, Macmillan, (1979).

Hodges, Jill and Hussain, Athar, 'Review Article on Jacques Donzelot's *La Police des Familles*', *Ideology and Consciousness*, No. 5 (Spring 1979).

Humphries, Jane, 'Women: Scapegoats and Safety Valves in the Great Depression', *Review of Radical Political Economics*, Vol. 8, No. 1 (Spring 1976).

Humphries, Jane, 'Class Struggle and the persistence of the working-class family', *Cambridge Journal of Economics*, Vol. 1, No. 3, pp. 241-258 (1977).

Kuhn, Annette and Wolpe, Ann Marie, editors, *Feminism and Materialism*, London: Routledge and Kegan Paul, (1978).

Land, Hilary, 'Women: Supporters or Supported?' in Barker and Allen, 1976.

Land, Hilary, 'Who Cares for the Family', *Journal of Social Policy*, July, 1978.

Land, Hilary, 'The Family Wage', *Feminist Review*, No. 6 (1980).

Lasch, Christopher, *Haven in a Heartless World*, New York, Basic Books, (1977).

Lenin, V.I., 'International Women's Day' *Pravda*, March 1920, reprinted in *Women and Society*, New York, 1938.

Malos, Ellen (editor), *The Politics of Housework*, Allison and Busby, (1980).

McIntosh, Mary, 'The State and the Oppression of Women', in Kuhn and Wolpe, editors (1978).

Merton, Robert K, *Social Theory and Social Structure*, Glencoe, Illinois: The Free Press (1957).

Milkman, Ruth, 'Women's Work and Economic Crisis', *Review of Radical Political Economy*, Vol. 8, No. 1 (Spring 1976).

Mitchell, Juliet, *Psychoanalysis and Feminism*, London: Allen Lane (1974).

Molyneux, Maxine, 'Beyond the Domestic Labour Debate', *New Left Review*, No. 116 (1979).

Reiter, Rayna R. (editor), *Toward an Anthropology of Women*, New York (1975).

Revolutionary Communist Group 'Women's Oppression under Capitalism', *Revolutionary Communist*, Number 5 (1976).

Rubin, Gayle, 'The Traffic in Women: Some Notes on the "Political Economy" of Sex', in Reiter (1975).

Seccombe, Wally, 'The housewife and her labour under capitalism', *New Left Review*, No. 83 (January 1974).

Seccombe, Wally, 'Domestic Labour and the Working-Class Household' in Fox (1980).

Smith, Paul 'Domestic Labour and Marx's Theory of Value', in Kuhn and Wolpe (1978).

Women's Publishing Collective, *Papers on Patriarchy*, Lewes, Sussex, 1976.

Invisible Struggles:
The Politics of Ageing

Florence Keyworth

My theme is the subjective experience of being an old woman. But first, it is necessary to state about old women in general one gigantic fact which overshadows the rest.

Old women are poor. Some two million old people receive supplementary benefit and over three million have an income which is at or less than 40 per cent above benefit level. That means well over five million elderly people live at or near the poverty margin. The majority of these people are women since women live longer then men. In a consumer society their poverty has a particular edge. Relatively few of them, for example, have cars. This fact you can see demonstrated any day in the supermarket as helpful assistants carry out cartons of goods to the car park for young customers while old women trudge off with their laden shopping trolleys.

Old women are very often badly housed. More than a quarter of the households whose members are aged sixty-five or more lack at least one basic amenity in the home – bath, inside toilet, hot water. Young people living in poor conditions can work and hope for better things. For the old, bad housing is usually quite literally the last place on earth.

When women cease to be sex objects because they are old, and when their children, now adult, are no longer dependent on their unpaid care, their value in our society slumps dramatically. Moreover, our society values individuals according to the size of their bank balances and their conspicuous consumption. Most old women have spent a large part of their lives doing hard, unpaid work in the home. In their employment outside the home, they have been grossly underpaid. So in old age they are poor. Unlike men, they very seldom get occupational pensions. They have no status and they flash no status symbols. Many old men are poor too, but old women are at the bottom of the pile.

My own position, therefore, is untypical. Married, but childless, I have been in continuous employment from the age of 17 and have been economically independent from the age of about 22. I draw a full single person's retirement pension, work part-time and live in a pensioner's bungalow – a minute brick hutch on a council estate. So, although many people would consider me to be poor, I am well off compared with millions of old women because, at sixty-two, I am still in part-time work and am decently if very modestly housed.

I write also as one of the 'young old' in the age range of about sixty to seventy-five, who, when healthy, are still physically mobile and able to enjoy wide-ranging activities. The 'old old' aged seventy-five and over, though often very alert mentally, are more likely to be hampered by physical infirmity and the loneliness it sometimes brings.

Elderly then, but not yet aged, and still working, I maintain, precariously, the position of a privileged old woman. That phrase 'old woman' keeps appearing on the page but it does not flow naturally from my pen. Contempt for old women stretches back down the centuries and, like other sexist attitudes, has become embedded in the language. The phrase 'old man' has a ring of affection. When young men use it in speaking to each other, it denotes amiability. For young women to address each other as 'old woman' would be unthinkable. The phrase is invariably an insult. To abuse a group of men and women, you must say 'old women of both sexes'. Think of the numerous terms for an old woman – hag, crone, old biddy, witch. Where are the male equivalents? In my youth 'wizard!' was an exclamation of high praise. However, let me, with some effort, acknowledge that I am an old woman who has had at least a decade to experience the way our society treats old women.

A few years ago, when in my mid-fifties, I had an experience which brought home to me the fact that I was now old. I was sent on a reporting job which involved a long wait outside a government ministry in order to interview a delegation following its meeting with a minister. Three young male reporters were also waiting. I had taken a book to read as we sat on the ministry steps. But the three young men amused themselves by observing each young woman who passed, commenting on her physical characteristics and estimating her likely performance in bed.

All this was accompanied by much giggling and falling about. At first, I thought they resented my presence and were doing this in an attempt to shock me. But as time passed, I realised the truth was something more disconcerting. They had not noticed me. I was invisible.

When old women are not invisible, they may be regarded as figures of fun or objects of contempt – as can be observed any day on television. There must be millions of women who, like me, have occasion to cringe inwardly almost every evening when watching the box. I sometimes think that if an observer from outer space learned about our planet only from the television screen, she could be forgiven for thinking the human race consisted mainly of the male sex and that females were a far less numerous sub-species with a life expectancy of about 40 years. Men engaged in sports, men pontificating on the political situation, men lecturing on arts and sciences, dominate the screen for hour after hour. Apart from a few women actors, the women on the screen are almost invariably young and beautiful. Male newsreaders, for example, can be grey-haired, balding, have bags under the eyes. Women newsreaders are young and flawlessly goodlooking. Old women don't exist.

In television comedies, any woman over forty-five is a figure of contempt – a twittering spinster or raucous mother-in-law. Stand-up male comics never tire of the mother-in-law joke. Another permanent joke is the one derived from the seaside postcard showing an old woman who is angry because her spouse is eyeing a younger woman.

There is immense social pressure to accept the image presented. If I join in the studio laughter when watching such shows, I feel I am betraying my sisters and myself. But the common attitude is that any woman who objects is prim and humourless.

The experience of old women is simply the end result of the sexism affecting all women. The old woman experiences sexism at its worst. She takes it neat, so to speak, undiluted by flattery or flirtation. But her situation casts its shadow backward over the lives of all women, even the very young. Women are conditioned to dread age, to look anxiously for the first wrinkle and grey hair in a way which would be considered neurotic in men. Their status is conferred on them by men. So when attractiveness to men is at an end, they become non-persons.

Economic independence is a good base from which to reject and challenge the appalling images which our society attempts to impose on us. But many old women are denied access to jobs and of those in work, many are forcibly retired at 60. Those in work are almost always in poorly paid, subordinate positions. They may have spent a lifetime in an industry or commercial undertaking, but they have been permanently barred from training for skill or management. This forces them to adapt to sexist assumptions which are so all-pervading that they are rarely challenged or even noticed.

A friend of mine once worked in the London head office of a large carpet wholesalers where a group of women secretaries in their fifties were taking dictation from young male travelling salesmen in their twenties and early thirties. These women often told the young men what to say in their letters. They knew a great deal about the firm's structure and stock, its customers and so on. These women had an attitude of maternal indulgence towards the young men who responded with jokey affection. The difference in their pay – the young men earned vastly more than the older women – was never mentioned. These women insisted they worked for a model employer and never questioned their place in the secretarial ghetto. They were, in fact, grateful that they had been retained in their jobs and not replaced by young women. They could not at any stage have done the young salesmen's jobs – not because of lack of drive, knowledge and potential, but because the competitive, convivial salesmen's world would never have accepted them. This shutter clangs down in front of women everywhere, whatever the job. It means that for all women, except a minority of highly qualified, professional people, work is always dead end. A woman at fifty has acquired skill, maturity, knowledge of the world. But she may well be stuck with the job she did at twenty and treated at best with kindly patronage because she is no longer young and pretty.

Since, for the past 36 years, I have been a *Daily Worker* and *Morning Star* journalist, my own work experience is hardly typical. Few women my age have the privilege of working in a place where any sexist remark is greeted by general howls of rage or derision. (This, by the way, occurs despite an appalling sex imbalance. Of more than thirty *Morning Star* journalists, only five, at the time of writing, are women.) Even so, at the *Morning Star* and within the Communist Party, I have, like others, encountered both the matter-of-fact comradeship which is what old women want in the work situation and the kindly condescension which is so infuriating.

Young women sometimes have a sexist-ageist attitude towards old women. These are narcissistic young women who have completely accepted our society's female stereotype. My experience here is limited, but I encountered some of them a few years ago when I took a shorthand refresher course. I was one of a group of women in their fifties in the class, most of whom were civil servants trying to get the formal qualifications which would increase their pensions. Some of the young women resented us. I remember hearing one describe us as 'those widows'. She appeared to think the word 'widow' was a disparagement. Rejecting us, these young women rejected their future selves and revealed a terrible insecurity.

Women's economic situation and the all-pervading sexism of our society can cause the ageing process to be bitter. Women in middle age – say early forties to late fifties – may face great difficulties. This is the age when many return to work after bringing up famiies – a step which may call for considerable courage.

It is vital for women in middle age – or at any age – to have a sense of personal worth based on skill and independence. This is difficult when independence is denied them and opportunities for gaining skills are few. By middle age, most women have acquired the skills, supremely important in human terms, which are needed in caring for children. But these skills are unpaid and are grossly undervalued.

Great resilience is often displayed by middle-aged women who cope with job-seeking at the same time as they face the emotional shock of marriage break-up. I have known women still caring for teenage children who, when their marriage has foundered, have taken unskilled work at poverty wages and have held the family together. 'I have come through all that and I am not afraid of anything life can do to me now,' one such woman told me. For women like her, conquest of personal catastrophe brings no status in our society, but it can eventually bring a realistic sense of worth.

These experiences may coincide with the menopause towards which quite barbarous sexist attitudes still exist. The menopause is still regarded as a fit subject for humour. Menopausal women are still sometimes treated with contemptuous pity. I am not competent to enter the controversy about the medical treatment of the menopause, but I am convinced that society's attitude towards it is a major problem, causing as much misery as the condition itself.

I was lucky enough to have sympathetic medical treatment during an uncomfortable menopause, but like millions, I rarely talked of it. I eventually wrote (anonymously) an article in which I described the experience of waking in the small hours, burning with heat and flinging off the bedclothes. I would sit on the edge of the bed as the sweat poured down, and beat off feelings of panic by staring at my watch and muttering: 'This will last six minutes and then subside ... ' I was amazed when one of the most reserved women I know, on reading this article, came over and embraced me. I had described her experience exactly.

I was able to write about the menopausal experiences of my fifties and I am now able to describe, I hope honestly, the subjective feelings of a woman in her sixties, because of the change in social climate which has occurred during the past ten years. This has been entirely due to the advent of Women's Liberation.

Old women are supposed to be jealous of the sexuality of young women. I sometimes feel the energy flashing from young women as if it were a visible rainbow. Am I envious?

don't think so. Young women and I live in different worlds and I am in a situation where these worlds overlap and interact from time to time in freedom and friendship.

It has been my good fortune during the last decade to work with young women who are feminists, and I know this is not typical. It has been a stimulating and unexpected experience. I am among the old women who welcomed with enthusiasm the development of Women's Liberation in the early seventies. It seemed to me then, as now, that young women were voicing thoughts which a few of my friends and I had had for decades. But their feminist analysis is deeper and much sharper than ours has ever been. Above all, they are speaking loudly and in unison as we never did. In our youth, there was no feminist movement with which we could identify.

The existence and work of young feminists has altered the behaviour of some old women, who at last are able to feel that they are part of a collective challenge to sexism, even though they are often surrounded by old men who are totally uncomprehending.

Recently I was at a pensioners' meeting where a male speaker referred repeatedly to 'pensioners and their wives'. Some of the women pensioners grew restive, feeling the same kind of anger which women workers feel faced with those continual references to the 'lads on the shop floor' uttered by male shop stewards. At last, one woman pensioner could stand it no longer. She rose to her feet and began to heckle. 'Women are pensioners too!' she shouted. 'Ah yes, the ladies, bless them!' he said. 'We couldn't do without them, could we?'

I have spent most of my adult life in the Communist Party. Some of its members, male and female, declare it has always been feminist in policy and outlook. My own view, on the contrary, is that the Communist Party still has to work towards becoming a feminist party, despite the excellent resolutions on women passed at its (overwhelmingly male-dominated) congresses.

My first encounter with Communism was in Sheffield in 1938 when I was in my late teens. I came from a stable but puritanical family and was conducting the usual search for truth after abandoning my nonconformist religion. 'Conquer

your future now!' said the Young Communist League posters
advertising an open meeting, due to be held in a room above a
pub. Many times a signatory of the teetotal pledge, I nerved
myself to enter licensed premises for the first time. I sat at the
back of the room while up front a group of young men argued
about some internal situation in the local branch of the
Amalgamated Engineering Union. No one spoke to me and
after listening in bewilderment for a time, I crept out –
perhaps before the meeting had officially begun.

Years later – about 1942 – travelling via the League of
Nations Union and the Left Book Club, I joined the
Communist Party in the company of two young women who
remained my closest friends until their recent deaths.
Sisterhood is not a new invention and I could not have become
a Communist without it.

We learned the jargon. 'District committee' meant the
Amalgamated Engineering Union, not the party. Women
were then barred from AEU membership. 'Barnsley Council'
meant the miners' leading body, not the municipality. The
miners were then, as now, a closed male community. In short,
the Communist Party was male-centred.

We studied Engels's *Origin of the Family* but were taught that
since capitalism is responsible for women's oppression,
priority must be given to the struggle for socialism,
achievement of which would automatically be followed by
women's emancipation. Impressive statistics about the
number of women doctors and engineers in the Soviet Union
were often quoted to prove the point. I can remember
believing that the Soviet Union had achieved full
emancipation for women and this gave depth to my political
enthusiasm. Many true and moving stories about Soviet war
heroines helped to strengthen this illusion – for illusion it
certainly was.

There was no searching discussion in the Communist Party
about women's oppression in Britain in the present. There
was some talk, but no real action, on equal pay. The need for
equal opportunity was largely ignored. As for women entering
the skilled manual trades, it hardly entered anyone's head.
Women's lot inside the home was a private matter which i

was unmannerly to mention. A few Communist Party women did voluntary work at a contraceptive clinic but kept rather quiet about it. It was not regarded as a political issue.

Sexist jokes and remarks within the party were common and taken for granted. In 1944, I attended in Rotherham a one-week party school where the students consisted of seventeen men and myself. 'Come on lads, don't a woman beat you,' said the tutor when I was answering questions at one point. He was a full-time district official of the party.

These attitudes persisted in the party and in the world at large despite the wartime role which women were playing in factories, farms and forces. The wartime Women's Parliament in which many Communist women played an important part, expressed a muted feminism. It was concerned with the provision of day nurseries and nursery schools and municipal restaurants, among other issues. In the early post-war years when the crêches and nursery schools were being closed *en masse*, there were some valiant campaigns against the closures, led by the National Assembly of Women. But throughout all these campaigns, women were encouraged by the Communist Party to regard themselves as 'relative creatures' – wives and mothers, concerned about peace, nurseries, rents and prices for the sake of their families.

One damaging result was that many Communist women (I was one) decided we were not interested in 'women's work' which we despised. We preferred to concentrate on the general political struggle and elected ourselves 'honorary men'. This led to arrogance, militated against sisterhood and helped to stifle feminist understanding. Communism, in my view, has yet to make its appeal to the core of women's consciousness. The centre of its stage is occupied by Man.

For women whose life pattern has been similar to mine, Women's Liberation has itself been liberating, enabling us not merely to articulate but to grasp completely thoughts which for decades have been half formulated. Economic independence has enabled us to welcome Women's Liberation whole-heartedly. But for this independence, women of my generation have usually paid a price – childlessness.

The millions of elderly women who have brought up

families have necessarily had to adapt to a male dominated society and many have accepted its ethos completely. Such women may feel intimidated by young women who seek a totally different life-style. They may feel threatened by the whole idea of Women's Liberation and erect mental barriers against it. This is understandable. Women of my generation cannot be expected to re-pattern their lives in ways which would endanger relationships with often much-loved husbands. An old woman may be well aware that her marriage is built upon decades of compromise and a hundred small pretences, but it may still be real and precious. Feminists sometimes give the impression that they are totally cynical about relationships with men. This is not a reflection of reality.

It is essential that young women approach these old women with understanding and some humility. What I mean is illustrated in the book *Dutiful Daughters* in which women of all ages, including the very old, tell of their experiences. The editors, Sheila Rowbotham and Jean McCrindle, approached old women with sensitivity and listened to them carefully. This was not done in a spirit of mere courtesy. They listened because they had a great deal to learn. Our society conditions many men to give no thought to personal relationships which they regard as women's sphere. Conversely many old women who have brought up families have developed down the years a very keen sensitivity in relationships. Their wisdom has no money value but is of great human importance.

Old age brings not only physical ills but emotional shocks. Although some tensions and anxieties recede, the alleged serenity of old age is largely a myth. Retirement may bring feelings of lost identity as well as a catastrophic fall in income. Close friends and relatives simply disappear one by one. through death, and life contains blank spaces where loved people used to be. The old woman whose fumbling slows you up at the supermarket check-out may be standing alone, or the edge of the world, gazing into the void. It takes courage to be old – more courage to be seventy than sixty, more courage to be eighty than seventy. This is the human condition. I affects men and women equally, though, since men tend to die first, it is the old women who more often face the final loneliness.

I have presented the old woman as victim. But old women are pretty tough and they are far less likely than young women to accept the images of themselves which society reflects back at them.

They have usually battled through difficult life situations. They know the value in human terms of the work they have done. There is often a sisterhood among groups of old women who have lived through similar hardships and who affirm each other's value. Personal friendships between women in age can be very rewarding.

Age brings to both men and women the realisation of how very brief is the whole span of past human history. When you have lived for the better part of a century, then 100 years seems no time at all. Changes which to young people seem to have been painfully slow, to us appear rapid. My grandmother, whom I knew for years, was born in 1855 when women had virtually no political or economic rights. All a wife's earnings were the legal property of her husband. Men could be seen lining up outside factories to take the women's wages from them on pay day.

My mother, born in 1882, was one of a plumber's fifteen children. She was forced to leave school at twelve to become a kitchen maid, but she had a burning ambition. She wanted to be a lady cashier, sitting in a glass cage and sending change along pulley wires to the counters of some smart shop. She actually achieved this ambition through her own special education. She would retire as often as possible to the privy down the yard – her version of 'a room of one's own' – and there set herself long tots. In her eighties, she could still add up figures with lightning speed – sometimes upside down across a counter – to the confusion of the Co-op assistants. She was clever, determined, full of potential. But her life consisted for the most part of grinding household drudgery.

Her own children were young in the inter-war period when it was considered shameful for married women to go out to work and when there were few jobs for them.

This history affects our thinking to this day. Now, when nearly half the work-force consists of women, married women often think of their earnings as belonging not to them but to the family – to be spent on the family. Men think of the money they earn as *their* money. So the idea of women's economic independence, taken for granted by today's feminists as an undisputed principle, is, in fact, a hard-won gain of relatively recent date.

My mother's struggle for self-fulfilment was a lonely one. Today, there is a rising tide of feminist consciousness. It is my good fortune to witness this in my lifetime and to feel myself a part of it.

'An Immense Verbosity': Permissive Sexual Advice in the 1970s

Rosalind Brunt

Sexual advice in the seventies starts from the premiss that a major change in attitudes has taken place in relation to the conduct and regulation of sexual activity. In this article I want to consider how that change is perceived by examining material drawn from the sex manuals of the period. For, as I will argue, I believe that these books have been important in contributing to what, now in the eighties, has become part of taken-for-granted commonsense wisdom about sexual activity. Because much of the prevailing sexual wisdom has been so oppressive and restricting to women in particular it has met with considerable challenge from the Women's Liberation Movement. Despite this challenge, the definitions established by the sex manuals in the seventies still remain part of the dominant discourse about sexual conduct in the eighties. I will be arguing that this has to do with the ways sexual advice assumes a liberal rhetoric of freedom, equality and consent and conveys it through a particularly plausible and persuasive 'tone of voice'.

Defining the parameters of 'sex'

There are two key terms in the definition of changed sexual attitudes: 'permissiveness' and 'sexual revolution'. Of course these predate the seventies, but it is only from the beginning of the decade, I suggest, that they achieve general and widespread currency and assume a dominance in the rhetoric of sexual advice. In the first instance 'permissiveness' implies the adoption of a relaxed, unshockable approach to sexuality – one that eschews morality because it is equated with rigid moralising. In the language of 'cool', permissiveness says: 'Everyone's doing it now, and so long as no one gets hurt, there's no big deal so don't get uptight.' Meanwhile the message of '*the* sexual revolution' is that changed attitudes are of enormous significance: 'sex' is the new gateway to an exciting life and the final bestower of individual identity and absolute meaning.

In looking further at the dimensions and contradictions of these terms for change, I will be taking examples mainly from advice addressed to women. This is because the seventies sex manuals all start from the assumption that all women are now sexually available to all men; because most of the books are framed in some kind of response, whether explicit or implicit, to what they (mis)recognize as 'feminism'; and because it is taken for granted that it is women, not men, whose sexual attitudes have changed in this period – or, if they haven't yet, then they are recommended, urged, indeed 'permitted' to 'do' something about it.

To start with the Foreword to a giveaway book of sexual advice published by the women's magazine, *Vanity Fair* in 1971. *Vanity Fair*, subsequently incorporated into *Honey*, was aimed at the late teens and early twenties audience of 'career girls'. This is the editor's introductory message to them:

> Life was safe and secure in the non-permissive age. And desperately, appallingly dull for many. Girls lived at home until they married suitably, or took a discreet job to mark time beforehand if they needed to. Lady Troubridge's guide, *The Book of Etiquette*, told you the correct way to behave and when to wear gloves, and the biggest problem was whether to have lace or satin for a wedding gown.
>
> Now, life isn't safe any more. It's adventurous, exciting, stimulating, precarious. There are fantastic jobs to be found, interesting flats to be furnished, foreign places to travel, your own car to choose and most of all, there are men who don't necessarily have only honourable intentions. You don't even *have* to wear gloves!
>
> So the old rules no longer apply. And the social and

professional niche you scrabble out for yourself is one you've worked for and won by your own efforts. This book is our way of helping you sort through the conflict of old-fashioned upbringing (which needn't necessarily equate with wisdom and sense) and contemporary behaviour.

Audrey Slaughter
Editor, *Vanity Fair*, 1971.

In these terms the *Vanity Fair* book announces to its audience that a change has taken place: they are entering a new permissive age where the rules of sexual conduct have been altered in a wholly beneficial and exciting direction. However, since they may still be confused by adherence to earlier, irrelevant attitudes, *Vanity Fair* will offer help by defining the new parameters. Beneath a cover photo of a young woman licking the nosetip of a man whose eyes are closed, the title of the book sets the terms: *Nice Girls Do: Vanity Fair's guide to the new sexual etiquette*.

The message of the title is borne out by the rest of the book. Henceforth sexual activity is to be defined not primarily as a moral question but a matter of contemporary *mores*, good manners, good taste. Desperately afraid of old-fashionedness, *Nice Girls Do* makes it clear that the questions for women are no longer those in the arena of principle: whether to, or not, or how far to – but belong to the etiquette of polite yes-saying to sexual activity and the men who supply it.

The terms are elaborated in chapter-headings like: 'A Philosophy of Considerate Adultery' or 'Twenty-five Things to Do for a Man in The Bedroom' ('Learn to make a bed with him in it. Buy him pornographic movies. Drink champagne together in bed – spill some on him and lick it off. Do not let mundane rituals interfere with passion. If he wants you now *now* now! at once! for heaven's sake, forget about brushing your teeth ... '). The woman being advised here is still in the image of the Sixties Chick, but the new decade has added a dash of 'Women's Lib' and the book has a section on 'coexisting' with 'our militant sisters' which actually advocates going along to a consciousness-raising group and reading up about feminism before you condemn it.

However, the accommodation with feminism remains an

uneasy one. It is the new availability of contraception, not the
women's movement, which is going to bring change. Most
importantly then, women should know about 'The Etiquette
of Not Getting Pregnant':

> Nothing is ruder – more cruel and careless – than an unwanted
> pregnancy ... That's why contraception is not only good manners
> – it's an expression of your wholesome lifestyle ... The pill is the
> Ultimate in Gracious Sexual Living – taken every day as
> automatically as you brush your teeth. The action is blissfully
> isolated from the act of love. How thoughtful. How considerate.
> How discreet. This is what etiquette is about.

At the beginning of the seventies then, *Nice Girls Do* signals the
notion that sexual activity has been evacuated from the realm
of ethical considerations and consigned to the arena of lifestyle
and etiquette. Throughout the decade, this is a theme
common to most books offering sexual advice. Its antecedents
are of course the Swinging Sixties, but why I'm concentrating
on the seventies in this article is because this is the decade
when sexual advice really 'takes off' in terms of mass
marketing and 'bestseller' promotion. And what interests me
about such massively available advice is how, in promoting
the idea of a current or recent change in sexual attitudes as a
shift from ethics to etiquette, the claim is made both that 'sex'
doesn't matter so much any more *and* that it is supremely
important. At one moment it is endorsed as part of the
mundane, everyday, 'like brushing your teeth' in *Nice Girls Do*
terms; at the same time 'sex' is promised as the sort of
ultimate personal fulfilment that 'everyone' is presumed to be
seeking.

Sexual advice as 'discourse'

But why consider advice *about* sexual activity? Why not start
by investigating real and actual sexual experience? With
adequate resources, using the methods of interview
questionnaire and personal account, it would of course be
possible to test the permissively-phrased 'ought' of the advice
books with the 'is' of people's own experience. Without those
resources, I would not claim that the 'ought' of pro-

posed sexual conduct, however permissively expressed, automatically coincides with the 'is' of sexual practices. But what I do want to suggest is that these books are likely to be influential as agenda-setters and worth examining seriously as ideological 'texts' in their own right. To take sex manuals seriously may still sound an odd enterprise, given that they're often regarded as a laugh, or testily dismissed as 'trash' along with boastful claims that no one ever needed to show *me* how to do it. But it's not only that their 'bestseller' status belies these jokey and anxious dismissals. I also believe that, given the social invisibility of sexual activity in our culture, the manuals' power-to-define will be a particularly forceful and authoritative one.

What is generally called 'sex' is a highly-mediated cultural phenomenon, directly experienced only by immediate participants, consigned to secrecy and privacy and not (usually, regularly) directly available to witness-by-others. Curiosity, desire for knowledge about the norms of sexual conduct, is thus primarily catered to not by immediate access but through the mediation of 'discourse'. 'Sex' enters the public domain as a topic to be talked about or visually and verbally represented – whether as 'pornography' in magazines film and video, various forms of 'erotica', the sexual 'confessions' of famous or fictitious people in newspapers and paperbacks, the sex 'quiz' in the popular press with 'self and partner ratings' and the various documentary texts drawing on popular psychology, medicine and commonsense with information on what to 'do' and how: the sex 'manuals'. This very discursive variety adds up to what Foucault calls 'an immense verbosity' about 'sex' in the culture. While exploiting it as *the* secret, he says, modern societies have at the same time 'dedicated themselves to speaking of it *ad infinitum*'.

From within this 'multiplicity of discourses', I'm concentrating mainly on the 'manual' type texts, which, typically, are mass-marketed first in the USA where they acquire a 'bestseller' tag that is then used to promote them in Britain, together with pre-publication serialisation in the popular tabloid press. They are written by two particular types of expert: the professional advice-giver, with qualifications in medicine, psychiatry, counselling; or the practitioner, whose expertise is based on immediate personal encounters. In the course of the texts themselves however it is usual to find both 'professional' and 'practitioner' claims being made.

These are claims to legitimacy, to being taken seriously by the reader. They are enhanced by forms of address which are the more credible for having a tone that is both authoritative and intimate. The reader's insecurities, both about sexual conduct and what other people 'do', are first invoked and reassurance is then offered in a 'voice' which recalls various forms of direct conversational speech. The readers are drawn into the 'conversation' in a way which encourages their consent. For the writers are 'with' the readers not only as supporters, but as if actually-present companions. Thus Dr Irene Kassorla invites her readers at the start of her recent manual, also called *Nice Girls Do*: 'And now it's time to take my hand and enter into your sexual adventuring. Together we will share in the loving experiences.'

This is a 'special relationship' set up in tones of between-ourselves privacy and offered to (presumed) anxious and curious readers, and is 'permissive' in the sense made current by the counselling therapies that burgeoned in the seventies: that of 'giving' permission to the 'client'. The idea is that the counsellor's clients already know what they most desire. What holds them back from pursuing their goals are repressions dating from childhood experience or fear of social disapproval. The role of the counsellor is to 'unblock' the client by expressing approval, emphasising the need to live in the present, take desires for reality. The apparent openness of this type of therapy ignores the extent of the counsellor's power to define the situation in the first place. Nonetheless, it provides a persuasive model for the transaction between writers and readers that is set up in the advice books. And while I have no means of investigating how people actually respond to reading them, I do suggest that these books offer considerable inducements to plausibility which in themselves make it worth looking more closely at some of their premisses and orientation.

Incitements to Sexual Fulfilment

The starting point of all seventies sexual advice is the assertion of every woman's right to sexual pleasure. She will be fulfilled as a person, and particularly as a woman through achieving her full sexual 'potential'. To be a real woman is to be a sexual woman – and this happens only via a male partner. Any other form of sexual pleasure, where it is considered at all, is either an inferior imitation or substitute for the 'real thing' and celibacy can only be defined as a lack, the worst form of missing out.

Given these premises, a new problem-category can be created: 'the sexually marooned woman'. Once created, this proves to be the category most in need of advice. The advice-giver who actually named the category is David Reuben, MD, author of *Everything You Always Wanted to Know about Sex (but were afraid to ask)*. This was the first of the sex manual blockbusters, a record in American hardcover publishing that sold 400,000 copies in three months of its appearance in 1969. When the British editions came out in 1970-71 the early gay movement campaigned against the book because of its extremely offensive remarks about male homosexuality – and indeed women. But David Reuben pursued his success by creating 'the sexually marooned woman' in his follow-up bestseller, *Any Woman Can!* first published in 1971.

The message in the title is similar in effect to *Nice Girls Do*. The problem is construed as a matter of women's inhibitions, which are preventing the expression of full sexual needs and drives. What the adviser has to do therefore is give women the necessary permission for release from self-repression. The book's subtitle explains its terms of reference: 'Love and Sexual Fulfilment for the Single, Widowed, Divorced ... And Married', and David Reuben's credentials as expert permission-giver are established at the start: 'With his usual informal wit and irreverent contempt for moral hypocrisy Dr Reuben offers a wealth of sound practical advice for women ... on how to improve their lives ... Using his years of experience as a psychiatrist and documenting his beliefs with detailed case studies, Dr Reuben tells women: How to beat society's practice of sexual repression and discrimination.'

The book makes a direct appeal to what Reuben believes to be feminism – the sort that is judged most in need of helpful male advice. It is written in the question-and-answer format that *Everything* ... first adopted – a familiar-ising 'tell me doctor' style that aims to reassure. It opens with a series of questions, as if from a naîve woman patient, who is simply assimilating and assuming the terms of an already defined problem:

> Chapter 1 The Sexually Marooned Woman
> *What is a sexually marooned woman?*
> Any woman who is unwilling or unable to fulfill her destiny as a fully-fledged female and thereby enjoy a lifetime of gratifying sexual experiences is sexually marooned ... A woman who is not completely expressing her womanliness in its most direct way is emotionally and sexually cut off from the rest of the world – *marooned.*
>
> Somewhere, somehow, something goes wrong. In America, the single woman is by far the most liberated member of society. Usually unfettered by children or family, often earning an excellent salary, glowing with good health, she has an abundance of free time to indulge her every whim, yet she often suffers under a terrible burden.
>
> *Which one is that?*
> The greatest of all human pleasures – sexual fulfilment – is officially denied to every adult female who is single, widowed or divorced. A woman is free to practise law, perform brain surgery, work on the hydrogen bomb, even travel to distant planets. She is morally – and in many cases legally – forbidden to merge her vagina with a penis, until and unless she marries.

Dr Reuben's therapeutic role here goes further than merely guilt-relieving; it contains a positive incitement to break the rules as he sees them. Rule-breaking involves a bold challenge to marriage as the main or only sanction for sexual activity. He tells women that the marriage licence has been a demeaning 'copulation permit' whereby the woman has been 'sponsored' by the man. Now he is giving women permission to be as extra- and pre-marital as they like.

However, it *is* still a copulation permit they are assumed to be seeking and Reuben's answers indicate that permissiveness has its limits. While marriage is no longer to provide the only allowable sexual opportunity, a rigid hierarchy of sexuality still remains. At its summit is 'the real thing', compulsively· heterosexual and genital. This is frequently referred to as 'normal' and 'mature' sex and ultimately legitimated by its most 'natural' function in reproduction. The sexual practices that marriage has always sanctioned are thus left unchallenged, nonproblematic. What sounds like a daring new vision turns out to be a familiarly reductive one. It all comes down to a penis-vagina merger in the end. Moreover, 'penis' and 'vagina' are hardly terms of equality. The sexually marooned woman is a male-defined problem and her body serves a male-defined function – just as, according to its original meaning, the 'vagina' is the scabbard that awaits the reentry of the sword. In the absence of the man with the penis, there can be no genuine female fulfilment and any other forms of sexual pleasure and erotic relationship are merely a pathetic joke.

In *Everything ...* , besides making plain the derisory nature of all homosexual relationships, Reuben had also stressed that celibacy did not even count as an option in the first place. Secure in the arrogant belief that 'celibacy' actually meant the same as 'no sex', he said, 'No sex is so stupid it is not even worth considering as a possibility.' What he now offers to women as the only sort of 'sex' that counts is first announced and celebrated as a positive human entitlement and then immediately specified as restricted to one particular activity which is further justified in the name of science. Thus: 'The most important principle to keep in mind is that sex is right. Human destiny is constant restless copulation, in spite of all the barriers and the obstacles. The instinctive compulsion to breed is irresistible.'

In this way, the 'permissiveness' that apparently denotes relaxed cool and bends back the rules in order to widen the gaps, now turns out to involve the frenetic corralling of sexuality to within the narrow boundaries of a fixed biological inheritance. And if it's back to reproduction in the end, why ever bother with contraception?

These final appeals to 'breeding' are commonplace in

sexual advice and the seventies manuals are no exception. But at first sight such biologism is curious because, besides displacing marriage, these books also announce the virtual abolition of sexual activity for the purposes of reproduction. The heroines of *Any Woman Can!* and *Nice Girls Do* do not refuse sexual marooning in order to have babies. They are precisely the women 'unfettered' by children: 'the single girls'.

The Single Woman and Sexual Consumerism

In their pioneer study of expert advice to women, Barbara Ehrenreich and Deidre English demonstrate a dramatic reversal of attitudes towards the 'single' woman that occurs in the sixties and seventies. From being associated with a lack and an absence – no men, missing-out, on-the-shelf, unfeminine, unattractive, frustrated, unfulfilled by children – she is elevated to a position of desirability, now the envy of the woman 'stuck' in marriage and motherhood.

Ehrenreich and English identify 'the rise of the single girl' in the USA and Western Europe particularly as marking a decisive break in the link between sexual activity and reproduction, and further, that between sexual pleasure and stable monogamy. Expert advice begins to downgrade motherhood and wifedom as the primary or only ideal goal for women and to celebrate the lifestyle of 'the single girl'. The first decisive expression of the shift is the 'defining' text: Helen Gurley Brown's *Sex and the Single Girl*, first published in the USA in 1962.

This title is rather misleading because the book is not specifically a sex manual nor even contains much sexual advice. It is rather to do with image-making, creating a transformation from negative to positive which is subsequently promoted as 'the *Cosmopolitan* girl' in the magazine Gurley Brown took over in 1965. By comparison with this image, say Ehrenreich and English, it is the mother/housewife who appears as the woman lacking and unfulfilled: '*only* a housewife.' Having been urged throughout the first half of the twentieth century by childcare experts, gynaecologists, psychologists, to find her true female essence in the subordination of self in child- and husband-centred nurturance, she now appears pathetically submissive, masochistically and parasitically dependent on home and husband to sustain her, secure in her nest but hankering after the lifestyle of 'the single girl'. By contrast, 'the single girl' is economically independent, has some kind of 'career' with surplus money to spend on herself, indulge her own leisure, and, most important, survive in the world of *men* – the majority of whom will be the masochistic housewife/mothers' husbands. Married men are 'fair game' for 'the single girl' because she doesn't at all seek to supplant the wife, merely to supplement her. While the wife provides the husband with 'home comforts', 'the single girl' gives him a sexually and intellectually stimulating good time and won't whinge nag and bore like the wife.

No wonder that a year after *Sex and the Single Girl*, Betty Friedan is describing 'the feminine mystique' in terms of the dilemma of women 'trapped' in the house and asking 'the silent question: "is this all?"' She calls it 'the problem with no name' because, why, when women now appeared to have everything they had apparently been born for, were they 'so restless, anxious, unfulfilled?'

One response to the problem is the political and collective one that results in the Women's Liberation Movement, with Friedan herself as a major activist. Through consciousness-raising, 'the problem' begins to get named and defined as shared by women-in-common. It is no longer some private individual neurosis that is 'all my fault really'. It is therefore open to challenge and change through the group practice of the WLM. But the other response is to remain in the realm of private neurosis and exhort the housewife/mother to emulate the individualism and competitiveness of 'the single girl' herself. As Ehrenreich and English show, the appeal here is to consumerism.

The single girls ethos fits well with consumerism because it extends the marketplace into the arena of sexuality. It emphasises the need to spend money on commodities that embellish and improve the body in the competition for getting and keeping men. Women at home are urged to enter and explore the market, for the price of marriage is no longer guaranteed security and relaxation, but continual vigilance.

An instance of how this message works is demonstrated in the way the mass weekly 'service' magazines for women like *Woman's Own* and *Woman's Realm* in Britain come to assimilate the Cosmo image in the seventies. Articles and advertisements appeal to women in the contradictory role of narcissist and domestic. They are required to be at one and the same moment self-involved, absorbed with body, clothing, hair, spending time and money in establishing a sexual identity as good as any 'single girls'' – *and* self-forgetful still, cheerfully abnegating themselves to the service of others in domestic labour. Trevor Millum's study of magazine advertisements of the period highlights these two trends. And contemporary magazine fiction often takes the resulting tension between narcissism and abnegation as its major narrative theme. The conflict produced in the woman protagonist's life is usually resolved by the declarations of her husband. He reconfirms her as a perfectly adequate wife and mother, and someone who can still excite him sexually: she hasn't 'let herself go', she is as 'good' as when she was single, only more so.

Working at Making It

But in the manuals of sexual advice no such conflict – even so 'magically' resolved – arises. Domestic labour and childrearing, if mentioned at all, are dismissed as so much dreary effort in comparison with the narcissistic task of making yourself over as a sexual being. For this alone will distinguish you in the eyes of a man:

> More than beauty
> More than brilliance
> More than great housekeeping abilities
> More than a model mother to his children
> He wants a Sensuous Woman ...
> Women who can clean, look good and mother children are a dollar a dozen, but a woman who can make a man feel his uniqueness is worth the world to him.

This is from the Introduction to *(How to become) The Sensuous Woman* by 'J' first published in the USA in 1969 where it sold a quarter of a million copies in six months and then marketed in

Britain from 1970 onwards, its bestseller status assured. Its unique selling proposition is that it is written by an enthusiastic 'practitioner'. It also offers the most clear-sighted definition of what a consumerist 'singles culture' requires in sexual terms.

The author, revealed in her next book, *Total Loving*, as Joan Garrity, a former book publicist who ran her own company, presents herself as exemplary: the single girl become sensuous woman. The point about the book is that the advice is based on 'J' 's own experience and extraordinary success-rate:

> This is definitely an 'unofficial' book by a laywoman (if you'll excuse the pun).
>
> An unbelievably happy laywoman, for as I lie here (I probably shouldn't admit it, but I write in bed) putting the finishing touches on *The Sensuous Woman*, next to me is the man I have always dreamed of but up until five years ago never stood a chance of getting.
>
> I won his love by becoming a Sensuous Woman and that's how I keep him coming eagerly home to me each night.
>
> To get him I did just about everything in this book. I know my method works even when the odds are stacked the other way, because you should have seen my competition! One rival looked like Grace Kelly and the other was the equal of Sophia Loren. Now I, on my best day, wouldn't be able to hold a mascara brush to the two ladies in question, who were also intelligent, charming and clever.
>
> Yet he left those two gorgeous creatures for *me*. Believe me it was no accident. A miracle, maybe, but an accident, no.
>
> I've gone ahead and built myself a truly beautiful sexual and romantic life and you, I believe with all my heart, will experience the same miracle of love and fulfilment if you follow the method in this book.
>
> Come on now. Get moving. You're going to have a wonderful time!

The form of direct address from 'me' to 'you' simulates the intimacies of conversation and invites assent from women readers. It evokes that flip, exaggeratedly 'feminine' style that is called 'gossipy' and occurs in a particular kind of writing for women: the comic account of domestic life regularly featured in women's magazines. And like the magazines, it appeals to a woman's custom of jokey self-deprecation. 'J' 's message is: if even *I* could do it, then certainly so can you, girls. For the point of her boast that 'some of the most interesting men have fallen in love with me' ('the producer of three of America's most popular television shows, a bomb expert for the CIA, a trial counsel, an apple grower' ...) is that 'you'd never believe it if we came face to face on the street.' Alongside the enumeration of her men she itemises her uglinesses. Not only is she unshapely and uncomely; other women can't even recognize her as a sexual threat. 'Unattractiveness' can be a good disguise:

> Mothers, wives and girlfriends think of me as the wholesome, apple-pie girl-next-door type (which, translated, means non-sexy).
> But while these mothers, wives and girlfriends are burning up over that spectacular-looking blonde undulating provocatively in the peekaboo leaopard print, I'm the one that's having the wonderful time – and getting and *keeping* men.
> For through intelligence and hard work, I have become a Sensuous Woman.

The exhortation to women readers to do likewise thus assumes that what we have in common is our feminine wiles. All-girls-together are addressed on the basis of what keeps us apart: the man-hunt. Bound together in an intimate conspiracy to prey on men we are also and always the rivals of our sisters.

The book therefore provides a manual of techniques for sexual predators and rivals. Tips from 'J's own experience are supplemented with anecdotes from women 'friends' about 'how to be a fabulous faker', 'how to tell in advance if a man will be a good bed prospect' and what to do 'when you hit a dry spell'. Answer: 'double your man-hunting activity, using both the General and Systematic man-hunting approaches. It won't be long before you hit real gold again.'

The language of the marketplace is apt because 'the most interesting men' also have the most economic pulling power. The sensuous woman techniques are the trade-off. If you work at them, like 'Vera' did in one of the success stories then you can 'hit pay-dirt right away'. The notion of being 'single' takes on the specific connotations of working as a 'lone operator'.

Regardless of whether a woman is actually married or not, she is 'free and independent', in the negative senses of being isolated and having responsibilities only to herself and for her own promotion in the sexual marketplace. And if the single girl/sensuous woman operation is 'about' achieving social and economic mobility primarily by sexual means, its accompanying rhetoric is that of 'the career'. How to construct a success out of sexual activity – 'making it' in every sense: 'You want to be a full woman don't you? Then down to business. We're marketing a product (you).' What the product costs is unremitting practice; systematic training in 'sensuality programmes', patience, dedication and strategic market-planning.

The vocabulary of sexual advice and its jollying-along tone exhorting women to keep 'making' and 'doing' it stands in marked contrast to that ideology which views sexual activity as spontaneous and natural. While 'J' may often refer to 'the miracle of love and fulfilment' she has no illusions that this miracle is an accident of fate. On the contrary, it requires prompt learning and the efficient acquisition of a wide range of social and physical skills. Furthermore, while all sex manuals claim that 'sex' is 'miraculous' in the sense that it is somehow transcendent, existing 'above' and quite apart from the material world of everyday economic preoccupations, the very concrete specifics of their advice suggest otherwise. For what they actually advocate in the way of sexual preparation and practice turns out to mirror precisely the world of work and the achieving disciplines associated with a protestant ethic of systematic and rationalised labour.

The advocacy of what could be called 'vocational sex', this compulsive concern with 'the hard work' that 'J' puts in to competitive self-improvement, has only one goal for a woman: to procure, pleasure, and most importantly, keep a man. The main motivation is economic: so that you can live off him.

The point prompts questions about the nature of the change that is assumed to have taken place through 'the sexual revolution'. The term implies something new and *therefore* different: a qualitative change is perceived. But what is being advocated here merely endorses existing male and female practices and leaves the man's class power intact.

Only a quantitative change is being proposed; more of the same is on offer. The advice is 'permissive' in the sense that it indeed 'permits', allows for, more interest in and expression of sexuality – but takes the existing cultural framework that binds class with gender as given and unalterable. To take an example, the sort of advice the contemporary sex manual is providing could not seem more remote from that conveyed in the 'moral tales' of the traditional love story written for women. But what both the manual and the romance are proposing turns out to be not really that different *in kind*. Constructed as models for feminine conduct, both the 'new' sensuous women and the heroines of romance have a vocational attitude to their sexuality. Their aim is to build a sexual career with the ultimate purpose of trapping those men whose superior economic status and resources goes with a barely controllable sexual appetite. In pursuit of the best lifestyle on offer, the sensuous woman must display a wide repertoire of sexual technique as her best exchangeable commodity; while the romantic heroine must conserve her skills and meantime use her virginity for barter. But this is a superficial distinction, for the message they both convey to women is the inevitable rightness of economic dependency on men.

However at the same time, the sex manuals are constantly proclaiming that their sensuous women are both independent of men and equal to them. What 'independence' and 'equality' mean in permissive discourse is revealed in the coy giveaway term 'liberated ladies': the women referred to are liberated only to the extent that they still remain ladies for the gentlemen. In this way, feminist aspirations for sexual liberation constantly get confused, equated and elided with the rhetoric of permissiveness. Sex manuals then go on to assert that of course we're all liberated now, that the goal of enlightenment has indeed been reached. Or rather, would have been, if there didn't remain one outstanding problem: women themselves. They (sic) are what makes sexual advice still necessary. Once women's heads have been sorted out with some help from the experts, they will be enabled to participate fully, joyfully and equally in that qualitative transformation of sexuality that is perceived to have taken place in the late sixties and seventies.

This is how Wendy Leigh describes her understanding of 'the sexual revolution' in her introduction to *What Makes A Woman Good in Bed* (1979), an advice book based on a series of interviews with mainly British and American celebrities:

> I grew up during the 'sexual revolution'. In 1955 a single girl was 'cheap' if she went to bed with a man. In 1965 she was 'frigid' if she didn't. And in 1975 almost every woman did. Whereupon men discarded the question: 'Does she or doesn't she?' (go to bed) and replaced it with: 'Is she or isn't she?' (good in bed). Sexual attitudes have altered radically – and my own childhood and teens reflected the resultant changes and confusion.
>
> I recognised that although female sexuality had theoretically been liberated and women's right to sexual pleasure conceded, full sexual freedom and the route to sexual pleasure was still inhibited in many women, because they tried to conform to a 'good in bed' stereotype.
>
> I decided to explore the subject further by asking men to define what *makes* a woman good in bed. I believed that the answers would provide commentaries on female sexual insecurities providing them to be either justified or invalid.

I think Leigh's rationale for her project provides another clear indication of where the boundaries of permissiveness lie. Although there appears to be some distancing from the notion of 'sexual revolution', as indicated by the inverted commas, the author does indeed think there's been a radical shift in both sexual behaviour and attitudes worthy the names of freedom and liberation. The remaining difficulty as she sees it is that *most women* don't yet appreciate the significance of the shift: they are still wary of entering their full sexual inheritance; they haven't yet relaxed into the idea sufficiently; they are still confused. The confusion arises because they do not yet realise how good men think they are in bed. The obvious answer therefore is that there should be more open discussion with men: this is how women will gain knowledge. Thus the 'solution' to their 'problem' is merely a restatement of it. The terms have not changed. For permissiveness views its 'independent woman' from within parameters so deeply male-defined they're hardly noticeable – and certainly not open to question.

All books offering sexual advice share a liberal view of knowledge: that simply to know more about what to do and how to do it will provide a way out of the current sexual confusion into the realm of freedom. As friendly guides and jolly but authoratitive exemplars, the function of the advisers is not to question the social context and parameters of that knowledge but helpfully to purvey it in an easily assimilable manner. But their very language betrays them. The terms and reference points of their sexual discourse indicate that the 'sex' they describe is all too closely bounded by the determination of class, ethnicity and gender.

The overt message of permissiveness is that 'sex' is an entity unto itself which transcends such determinations.It is the 'essence' of self-fulfilment, a force for good in the world that is always and only life-enhancing and therapeutic. Accordingly, 'the sexual revolution' assumes an abstract, idealist, almost spiritual, power which is to be counterposed to the awfulness of real material existence. From this persepective, the advice-givers exhort readers to celebrate the transformative happiness properties of 'sex'. At the same time, they cannot help but reveal that the values of 'sex' remain stubbornly rooted in the cultural and material practices of the everyday world.

I want to examine such 'contradictions' with reference finally to *The Joy of Sex*. I've chosen it last because, as the title indicates, it contains the most elaborate celebration of a permissive approach and resumes many of the themes I've already raised. It is also the best bestseller of the period. Indeed, it continues to sell in the eighties and could be called 'the classic text' of permissiveness in the sense that its probably the most influential and comprehensive agenda-setter of all contemporary sexual advice.

Fantasy and Coercion

The Joy of Sex was first published in the USA in 1972 and has sold over seven million copies to date. Its unique selling proposition was, and remains, the range of sexual practices it advises on. Together with its sequel, *More Joy of Sex* (1977) it also trades on its association with Alex Comfort, a name that stands for relief from the 'anxiety-makers' and all forms of sexual repression. The actual authors, a married couple, are anonymous because one is a doctor. Comfort is described as their editor and is well-known as a biologist and medical expert and campaigner for liberal causes.

The book is aimed at what is called 'the couple', assumed to be heterosexual and stable – and most importantly, without children, or, in this context, 'childfree'. As Ellen Ross has pointed out, the theme of the couple-without-children predominates in seventies advice books and *The Joy of Sex* takes some trouble to justify its position. It is a campaigning book and one of its missions is to promote 'high-grade sex' and get it widely recognised as a full-time leisure activity, indeed, the most therapeutic form of adult games-playing. This aim involves the most radical break from procreative sexuality. Not only are the two types of sexuality basically incompatible in purpose, it is highly irresponsible to try and make the best of both. A choice must be made, for 'the sort of sex we ... are talking about here almost excludes fertility'. So, 'frankly, unless you're prepared to make concessions, stick to sex and don't have children'.

'High-grade sex' needs dedicated followers. They cannot be subject to interruption when they launch out on the activity which is to be the ultimate grown-up hobby. The context of this 'sex' is clearly established within the sphere of consumption. It matches Ehrenreich and English's point about the 'singles culture' and its rapid penetration of 'the couple' lifestyle in the seventies, and how it encourages opposition to maternalism and reproduction in the name of active leisure and consumerism.

Hence the class-assumptions that sell a lifestyle. Throughout *The Joy of Sex*, appeals are made to the reader through the medium of good taste. This is to be 'the first explicitly sexual book for the coffee table' and sexual joy is metaphorically compared with what goes on in the worlds of concert-going, opera and ballet and the appreciation of fine wines. But the most extended analogy is with conspicuous culinary arts. On its cover, the book is described as a 'Gourmet Guide to Lovemaking' and it turns out that this is to be 'an haute cuisine Cordon Bleu' sex manual. The originality of the joke is indeed what leads Comfort to lend his name to it:

> The basic idea struck me as unique. A cookery book is a sophisticated and unanxious account of available dishes – culinary fantasies as well as staple diets – with the practical details provided. This book is an equally unanxious account of the full repertoire of human heterosexuality. As such, it is long overdue. A cookbook tells the novice how to tackle a live lobster, what to do when the mayonnaise separates, how to fix a chateaubriand. The authors of this book describe in the same unruffled detail, and with a sense of fun, what to do about impotence or premature ejaculation, how to manage oral sex, how to play symbolically aggressive games, how to treat a partner who is hip for 'discipline', how not to be bothered by fetishes, how to use kinky clothes as sex stimuli ...

I'm not convinced about the 'sense of fun' and lack of anxiety. The lighthearted humorous style of the book that Comfort refers to betrays a tone of desperate trendiness, an edgy concern to establish the fine trademarks of class and style. As in the other sex manuals, jokeyness apparently confirms the special relationship between writers and readers and emphasises intimacy. But it also implies a sense of distance, and particularly when they're at their most flip and facetious, the advice-givers betray a nervy unease with their subject matter. *The Joy of Sex* is Comfort's project for releasing sexual 'hangups' and 'blockages' but it addresses its readers in the voice of a guilty voyeur.

Sustaining this joke that is in earnest, the book is divided into Starters, Main Courses, Sauces and Pickles and Problems. It is illustrated with two types of material: a centre insert of oriental 'erotic art' in colour plates; and tasteful line drawings of a young, vaguely hippy-looking couple in a variety of poses to accompany the text. But the young couple's positions are tasteful to the point of blandness and actually bear little relation to the text.

This is because the book is dedicated to 'uninhibited frankness' with the specific claim that it is rescuing certain sexual practices from the repressive underworld of kinks, guilt and pornography and consigning them to their rightful place within the celebratory general category of 'sex'. They are to be restored under the beneficial new light of permissive sexuality. For 'the couple' invoked by the book is in the liberal Wolfenden mould of 'consenting adult in private'. And if 'frankness' is really working for them, and they've taken the author's advice on excluding children and equipping the bedroom as a private sexual gymnasium, then all that matters is whatever turns them on so long as they both agree. Permission is granted: 'What is "normal" is what you both enjoy. There are no rules.'

In fact there are plenty and liberalism is exposed as threadbare. The permissive world the couple is invited to enter is much more dense and 'filled-in' than the vague line drawings would suggest. The new and modern is once more the old and familiar. Their world is actually a re-presentation in contemporary guise of the familiar colonialists' bordello and the couple's guide is the connoisseur of the place, a world-weary but refined gentleman – the Victorian Sensualist.

The tone is predominantly that of one colonial gentleman addressing another. The woman author's voice is mainly silent in the book and the man is the main subject of the text. The content is mainly about what 'he' can do 'to her' or the way in which 'he' can be serviced 'by her' – described in a men-only conversational tone: '*Stockings* – Can be a sexual turn-on – often the preferred ones aren't the fashionable kind but the old-style black stockings which look prossy. Tights are an obstacle unless crutchless, and only erotic, for most males, if worn without panties, and then chiefly visually. It is said that if you can get one stocking off her you're home.'

In the mouth of the modern authors, the Sensualist tells the couple of 'the bordel tricks' he has learned in his travels and accords them their proper French names – *cassolette, croupade, cuissade, flanquette, feuille de rose*. More exotically, Viennese Oysters, Turkish Harems or South Slav style are evoked, accompanied by the sort of travellers' tales that get retold in the clubs of the gentlemen. So South Slav style is: 'mock rape – you throw her down, seize one ankle in each hand and raise them over her head, then enter her with your full weight ... The style is passionate and affectionate as befits a race of bridestealing warriors whose women were formerly, and still are, natural partisans, tough plus tender.' Or there is: '*A La Nègresse* – from behind. She kneels, hands clasped behind her neck, breasts and face on the bed ... Very deep position – apt to pump her full of air which escapes later in a disconcerting manner.'

The authors' project is to rescue pornography. In the process, the racist and imperialist elements of pornography are preserved – indeed, rehabilitated, through the apparently guilt-free language of 'cool'. The coolest sex-game derived from pornography is bondage. And just as the social context of the book is the imperial bordello, so bondage proves to be its main frame of reference.

The piquancy of being tied or tying up, 'laying' or 'staking her/him out' is advocated throughout and here the dislocation between the visual and verbal material is most marked. For the centrality of bondage to the written text is nowhere conveyed in the line drawings – apart from two discreet illustrations displaying fragile dinky bows round arms and ankles. The authors are clearly aware that their advocacy may prove controversial. When bondage is transferred from Victorian pornography and sanctioned as respectable in a sex manual, it is therefore necessary to refer to the celebratory view of sexual activity: its justification must be in terms of the utopian world of transcendence, play and lifestyle fantasies. And because bondage then appears to have no obvious relation with 'real life' it cannot be interpreted as a moral issue.

Accordingly, the authors emphasise the importance of acting out and not repressing or 'blocking' your sexual fantasies because, 'This is a dream you are in.' Furthermore, because you remove bondage to the realm of play and consign it to the privacy of the bedroom you might actually reduce the likelihood of 'real-life' atrocities. With this echo of the cool 'make love not war' slogan they go on to suggest that bondage used as therapy might indeed serve to prevent genocide, because: 'People who act similar aggressions outside the bedroom are apt to end up at My Lai or Belsen.' So once the bedroom has been sanctified as quite separate and shut-off from such situations, the authors need not enquire what determining aspects of 'real life' might have provided the turn-ons for bondage fantasies in the first place.

The bondage menu proper comes in the Sauces and Pickles section of the book where its main function is said to be the absolute attainment of uninterrupted sexual release. It is best practised in conjunction with a particular technique of slow masturbation by partner which the authors recall was perfected in the real conditions of colonising the gooks: 'The domestication of this experience, which veterans will recognise as the Japanese-massage-special-treatment routine, may be the one good thing America gets out of the Vietnam war.' But it's only because this routine is so unbearably pleasurable that it is just most advisable to do it not merely tied up, but securely staked-out, gagged, blindfold – and if you like, dressed-up. If played 'fairly' and according to the Federal Safety Code to avoid death and injury, this is a *gentle* game, 'not kinky or frightening – just human.'

In this book imperialism always wears a human face – whether it's that of the Victorian Sensualist or the American GI getting sexually serviced by the women of nations they've subjugated. But besides its specifically colonial connotations, bondage has another meaning when it's the woman who's been tied up. Especially if the gag is worn: 'As one lady put it, "it keeps the bubbles in the champagne." Gagging and being gagged turns most men on – most women profess to hate it in prospect, but the expression of erotic astonishment on the face of a well-gagged woman when she finds she can only mew is irresistible to most men's rape-instincts.'

There is no mistake about these 'instincts'. The 'theory' behind the book is derived from the reactionary concepts of sociobiology which became highly influential in the seventies and were constantly challenged by feminists for positing a rigid biologistic account of gender differences. In particular, *The Joy of Sex* acknowledges its debt to Desmond Morris, whose account of sexuality in *The Naked Ape* underpins the whole joyful enterprise. Morris' writing betrays a phallocratic obsession: his view that the penis is the motor force of history bestows on him a mission to remind people that while 'homo sapiens is pleased that he has the biggest brain of all the primates (he) attempts to conceal the fact that he also has the biggest penis.' What the naked ape uses it for, Morris insists, is inevitably, relentlessly, and for all time, to prop up the pair-bond and maintain his property-rights with the violence of the hunt and the territorial imperative.

Running on the same biologistic lines, *The Joy of Sex* proclaims an essentialist message that – yes, there may be endless sexual permutations and varied 'menus' to cook up; and yes, 'everyone's into role-swapping now' *but*, underneath, and when it comes down to it, there are only two basic human natures, each biologically 'programmed' with two distinct sexual responses, those of subject and object, of dominant and dominated. And it's these natures, fixed and innate, which are relentlessly played out in the fantasy games of bondage that the book describes: Burglar and Maiden, Sultan and Concubine, Master and Slave.

The woman author of the book attempts to assert something different – albeit sounding rather flip and still using the language of cool. In a section, 'Women (by her for him)' she says, 'the old idea of man as raper and woman as rapee being built-in is contrary to all experience. As to the Women's lib bit, nobody can be a good lover – or a whole man – if he doesn't regard women as a) people and b) equals. That is really all there is to be said.'

But her voice is overruled by the combined male voice of her husband, Comfort and the sociobiologists. In the section, 'Men (by him for her)', women are told:

> Male sexual response ... is triggered easily by things, like putting a quarter in a vending machine. Consequently, at a certain level and for all men, girls, and parts of girls, are at this stimulus level unpeople. That isn't incompatible with their being people too. Your clothes, breasts, odor, etc., aren't what he loves instead of you – simply the things he needs in order to set sex in motion to express love. Women seem to find this hard to understand ... The Women's lib bit about sex objects misses the point – sure the woman and the various parts of her are sex objects, but most men ideally would wish to be treated piecemeal in the same way. Accordingly, the most valued thing, from you, in actual lovemaking is intuition.

Just as *The Joy of Sex* presents itself as the last word in permissiveness, it should not be surprising that it is the male voice and masculine values that predominate in the end. Nor indeed that the final bedrock of permissiveness should prove to be a vision of sexuality that is male-defined and makes the appeal of 'back to basics'. For at the very moment that the range of the normal and acceptable seems to be 'permitted' an extension, it is actually being restricted and closed down within the boundaries of 'intuition', 'instincts' and biological inheritance. Apparently given the sanction of natural science, the existing inequality between women and men is justified on the grounds of timeless sexual urges. And what *The Joy of Sex* confirms is that ultimately what 'biology' urges men to do is be violent towards women. The male authors would of course disclaim that. After all, incitement to violence takes place in the realm of fantasy and play. It isn't real. And yet they are also telling their readers that violence conforms exactly to the dictates of a man's essential sexuality and that it is literally bondage that keeps the pair-bond together, just as they are, for ever.

For all that the term 'permissiveness' implies consent, I would suggest that the way it is applied in the advice of the sex manuals is indeed coercive. Although extreme, the incitement to sexual violence in *The Joy of Sex* is not actually an exception to the type of advice that is generally on offer in the sex manuals. I would claim – and I hope I have given some evidence of this through quotation – that the whole framework of permissive sexual advice is coercive in the sense that its vision of sexuality is compulsively rigid, monolithic and reductive. As Foucault emphasises in his study of sexuality, 'power' and 'discourse' are closely enmeshed. Sex manuals use their peculiarly strong power-to-define first in order to limit what counts as 'sex' and then to establish what constitute 'the problems' and 'the solutions' in sexual conduct. The advice is so given that to refuse the categorizations is to risk being defined as an unjoyful, no-saying and non-sexual person and, given the sex manual's insistence on the absolute identity of sexual and personal fulfilment, maybe not a person at all.

However, as I've also tried to indicate, the coercive element of permissive discourse does not appear to be the dominant one in sex manuals precisely because the language and 'tone of voice' of the discourse is so persuasively cool and consensual. It establishes the special relationship between advice givers and takers that betokens an intimate equality. It would be almost rude for readers to refuse the terms.

Rude voices of feminism

But there are rude people about, especially feminists, and, as I've said, permissiveness does have its contradictions. I suggest that it is indeed on the basis of these contradictions and arising out of a critique of permissiveness that the women's movement has begun to develop versions of what might become 'an alternative sexuality'.

In 1974 the Women's Liberation Movement adopted the following demand at its national conference in Edinburgh: 'An end to discrimination against lesbians; the right to our own self-defined sexuality.' Subsequently, many feminists felt that the two aspects of the demand did not coexist very easily and that the second part was obscuring the anti-discriminatory appeal of the first. Therefore at the last national WLM conference, in Birmingham 1978, we decided to keep the first part as the whole demand and to adopt the second part as a *principle* of the movement, placing it at the head of all the demands as a preamble to them, thus: 'Women's Liberation asserts the right of all women to a self-defined sexuality.'

Starting from the position of the demands and the principle, the women's movement makes clear that our sexuality is not an immutable Fact of Nature. Although we recognize its biological basis, we consider sexuality to be primarily a matter of social and cultural construction and *therefore* open to change through collective self-determination. Further, that the women's movement should inscribe sexuality into a statement of *political* aims points to our recognition that it cannot be divorced from considerations of power. We interpret gender relations as relations of power and pose a critique and challenge to the way they currently determine and circumscribe our sexuality.

More specifically, when it comes to interpretations of sexual *activity* and *conduct*, there are no feminist equivalents of the permissive sex manual. For one thing, we don't set ourselves up as expert advisers and practitioners. But in any number of small-group discussions, workshops, conferences, and now some books (1) we are exploring sexual possibilities from a politically conscious perspective. I would describe the aim of this sexual politics as being 'about' both disrupting existing sexual categorisation and expanding the range of the erotic.

I cannot 'sum-up' a discussion that is only in its opening phases and is anyway about potentials and about the processes of building alternatives. But it is already clear that our demands are about autonomy and choice and for a 'sex' that is more than instrumentalist 'fucking'. We are therefore challenging the heterosexist supremacy of the penis-vagina merger in which the penis figures as the penetrative weapon of the hunt. We also question the goal-oriented vision of the final coming, the mutual orgasm that is somehow 'given' not made. Notions of a feminist sexuality start from the clitoris, rather than the vagina-in-waiting, as the source and centre of women's sexual pleasure. But what feminists also say is that the erotic is by no means exclusively located in the sphere of 'the genital'. It is more to do with taking pleasure and pride in the whole body.

The idea is most cogently expressed in the recent feminist book, *For Ourselves* which demands a new appropriation of 'making love'. It is significant that in permissive discourse this term has become increasingly restricted and that in common currency it has come to act as a coy euphemism for 'straight fucking'. What *For Ourselves* proposes is a whole widening-out of the definitions of 'making love'. In the first place it is to be about self-love in the dual sense of self-esteem and self-pleasuring. And only when we take pride in 'our bodies, ourselves' are we able – but only if indeed *we* wish it – to take pleasure and enjoyment in the bodies of others. In this view, lovemaking is an actively tactile experience in which the compulsive separation between excitement and tenderness is broken down.

Like the woman author's voice in *The Joy of Sex*, the voices of feminism are still too often 'talking to each other'. Not by a long way have the new definitions of our sexual politics even begun to attain widespread currency throughout the culture.

But I do suggest that the present feminist debates already show possibilities for eventually out-talking the permissive and patriarchal discourse of the sex manuals. If for no other reason than that women are, by nature, more verbose.

Note 1

Examples of relevant books are:
Boston Women's Health Book Collective, *Our Bodies, Ourselves*, British edition by A. Phillips, J. Rakusen, Penguin Books, London 1978; A. Coote, B. Campbell, *Sweet Freedom*, Picador, London, 1982 – particularly the chapter on 'Sex'; S. Hite, *The Hite Report: A Nationwide Study on Female Sexuality*, Tamly Franklin Ltd., London, 1977; S. Hite, *The Hite Report on Male Sexuality*, Macdonald Futura, London, 1981; A. Koedt, "The Myth of the Vaginal Orgasm", 1970, reprinted in *Radical Feminism*, edited by A. Koedt et al, Quadrangle Books, New York 1975; A. Meulenbelt and others, *For Ourselves: Our Bodies and Sexuality from Women's Point of View*, English edition, Sheba Feminist Publishers, London, 1981.

References

H. Gurley Brown, *Sex and the Single Girl*, Giant Cardinal edition, Pocket Books, New York, 1963.

A. Comfort (ed.), *The Joy of Sex*, Simon and Schuster, New York, 1972.

A. Comfort (ed.), *More Joy of Sex*, Quartet Books, London, 1977.

B. Ehrenreich, D. English, *For Her Own Good*, Pluto Press, London, 1979.

M. Foucault, *The History of Sexuality, Vol. 1 An Introduction*, Allen Lane, Penguin Press, 1979.

B. Friedan, *The Feminist Mystique*, Penguin Books, London, 1965.

'J' *The Sensuous Woman*, Mayflower Books, London, 1970.

'J' *Total Loving*, Mayflower Books, London, 1978.

I. Kassorla, *Nice Girls Do*, Granada Publishing Ltd., London, 1981.

W. Leigh, *What Makes A Woman Good in Bed*, Mayflower-Granada Publishing Ltd. 1979.

T. Millum, *Images of Women*, Chatto and Windus, London, 1981.

D. Morris, *The Naked Ape*, Triad Mayflower Books, London, 1977.

D. Reuben, MD, *Everything You Always Wanted to know about Sex ...* W.H Allen, London, 1970.

D. Reuben, MD, Any Woman Can! W H Allen, London, 1972.

E. Ross " 'The Love Crisis': Couples Advice Books of the late 1970's", in *Women, Sex and Sexuality*, C K Stimpson and E Spector Person (eds) University of Chicago Press, 1980.

Sexual Politics and Psychoanalysis: Some notes on their relation

Rosalind Coward

We have reached a critical moment in the Women's Movement when the issue of sexual politics has been revived with a new kind of urgency. This urgency derives both from increasing acts of public aggression towards women and the simultaneous increase in women's awareness of these acts. It also derives from a new determination within the Women's Movement that we have strategies towards these phenomena, strategies which might ultimately mean that we also have to examine our own sexual identity and choices. In such a context it would seem that there is a very great need for careful investigation of what we mean by sexuality and sexual identity, as well as a careful assessment of the source of the problem and the possibilities for change.

Heterosexuality. The conscious choice?

The question of sexual choice and identity, defined in terms of who you sleep with, has become central to discussions about sexuality. In particular it has been bound up with discussions about how sexual relations between men and women can be changed. The Women's Movement has been concerned not just over the last fifteen years, but historically, with problematizing sexual relations. Over the last few years, though, there has been something of a shift in emphasis. The recent call from revolutionary feminists has been for a total critique of heterosexuality. This call has renewed a politics destined to challenge sexual engagement with men as a necessary strategy to produce changes in masculine behaviour.

The current offensive has as its object 'heterosexism' viewed as the practices and ideologies which produce the heterosexual imperative. It draws attention to the way in which not only the family but violence against women and representations of women are connected in their effects. They ensure that women's sexuality is organised into heterosexuality, in which men dominate and women are subordinate.

This position within the Women's Movement has by no means met with unequivocal acceptance. Many women feel anxious about its implications. For the critique of 'heterosexism' has produced a new imperative to examine exactly what are our relations with men. It has suggested that the form taken by our relations with men can never be changed while sexual engagement remains unchallenged.

At the heart of the anxiety are a number of unresolved questions. Is it the act of intercourse with men which perpetuates the dependency on which certain cultural presumptions work? Or does this dependency arise from the structures of desire and expectation surrounding the sexual act in a culture such as our own? Or is it that men consciously pursue their own interests, and that sexual subservience is the primary means by which these are secured?

In such a context there is clearly some need for clarification of whether we are challenging men as 'source' of our subordination, and whether a critique of heterosexuality implies a rejection of it. This question has been largely posed with bitterness and answered with a silent defensiveness neither of which is at all surprising. On the one hand, it has been posed in a way which seems to neglect previous discussions of the form taken by sexual subordination and its relation to other forms of oppression in our society. On the other, it is a challenge to that aspect of ourselves which we regularly take to be the most hidden, and therefore the truest expression of our identity, that is, our sexual needs and activities.

For this reason many of the political statements about

sexual activities, far from offering ready solutions, appear to cause some discomfort. It has become clear that although earlier feminist discussions failed fully to challenge the effects of masculine behaviour, contemporary discussions are insensitive to the depth and contradictoriness of our sexual needs and emotions.

The extent of these contradictory feelings can be gauged by considering this difficult problem. No feminist would deny the need to challenge masculine sexual behaviour when it takes the form of violence, even hatred of women. However, many women are loath either to name men in general as the intentional agents of such violence and hatred, and, more especially, loath to sever all emotional and sexual involvement with men.

What means, then, do we have at our disposal both to understand and critique the forms which sexuality takes within our culture? To some extent this question is evocative of discussions which have always haunted feminism. Where does women's subordination reside? In legal, economic or political practices whose effect is to force women into emotional dependency and subordination? In ideologies which structure women's emotional life and expectations and guarantee that other social practices can operate? And what underlies these practices? Is it an economic and political structure equally oppressive to a number of social groups deprived of any control? Or are all these practices only operative on men's literal and brutal control of women through the expression of masculine sexuality?

Given the way in which these discussions have been revived, it seems that some of the solutions found earlier to these questions are slightly unsatisfactory. Socialist feminism, in a very proper insistence on the complexity of a social formation structured around multiple contradictions, has nevertheless seemed to absolve men and shirk the issue of dominance within sexuality. We seem to be revisiting certain discussions perhaps because of a failure to advance our theorization of the subordination. There seems to be a need still for a more sensitive approach to the question of sexuality, one which would insist on masculinity as a problem but would not reduce the complexity of social relations to a simple power struggle between men and women, in which we stand and fall over whether or not we have sex with men. This would not be a matter of letting men off the hook but of finding a way of understanding subordination in the sexual domain without abandoning the perceived complexity by which choices and identities are structured.

There are two central issues in the current 'round', both of which I think can be helped along by psychoanalytic theories. One is the way in which the discussion of heterosexuality has fallen out around the issue of whether or not we hate men. The second is the theorization of the sexes as interest groups. On the first point, which is at the root of much feminist dis-agreement, it seems necessary to re-emphasise that what is at stake is not our individual response to men, but our response to a culture which hates women and feels profoundly ambivalent about expressions of a female sexuality. In such a context what is required is a means of investigating ideological forms and forces through which masculinity and femininity are constructed.

On the second point, there is equal urgency to reiterate criticisms of the idea of the sexes as interest groups. Most feminists would agree that the conscious intentions of individual men are less relevant than the fact that society ascribes different possibilities of power according to your position in diverse practices. However progressive their politics, any white person is in a structurally different position to any black person in a racist society. Good intentions and liberal conscience in no way affect this, although alliances between progressive groups may have a role to play in fighting racism or sexism. But in spite of a level of agreement on the irrelevance of intentions, some feminists do still argue as if direct male interests were served by the social control of women. It is difficult to know what these interests might be, unless we are to fall back on some unexamined notion of a psychologistic urge for power.

Both these aspects could in fact be profitably rethought with a more elaborate notion of social structure and the workings of power and violence within the sexual sphere. But to suggest that men have a psychological imperative to control and harm women implies that women must retreat from men to a realm of safety where our own needs and desires can be discovered. This of course is a hard if not impossible solution for those women who might feel that their needs and desires might include men, however problematic that 'choice' may be.

Psychoanalytic discussions, both of the cultural forms assumed by sexual relations and of the identities and structures of desire produced in these forms, suggest a more searching approach. Some of the investigations conducted within a broadly psychoanalytic approach have the potential to help us understand our heterosexuality rather than just reject it. What's more, this understanding does not lead to complacency but to some extent seeks to free us from compulsions and investments which can destroy us.

Psychoanalysis insists on seeing the formation of our sexual needs and emotions as a process in which conscious and intentional activity has only a very small part to play. This is in direct confrontation with the usual ways in which we understand the social structure and the actions of individuals within it. Psychoanalysis proposes ways of investigating the social structure as a particular kinship and familial organisation whose imperative is upheld in the psycho-sexual construction of individuals.

It might be asked whether psychoanalysis is just another account which proclaims men innocent since it insists on understanding the investments which both sexes have in the forms taken by sexuality in our culture. On the contrary, I think psychoanalysis has a way of understanding the construction of the individual which can neither be ignored nor comfortably integrated with previous ways of seeing the social structure. Far from absolving men, it points to ways of understanding masculine sexuality. It reveals a particular compulsion which our culture has towards female sexuality, and it hints at the deep hold which this compulsion has for the identification made by both men and women. Importantly, psychoanalysis is a theory which insists on the absolute centrality which this society ascribes to anatomical distinction. Psychoanalysis attempts to delineate the psychical consequences of this anatomical distinction but at the same time refuses any indissoluble link for example between 'femininity' and the anatomical female. All these claims are premissed on psychoanalysis's most significant claim, the claim that conscious intentions are a tiny part of our being and that the unconscious and its investments have to be investigated.

Identity in Psychoanalysis

> Only since Freud have we begun to suspect what listening and hence what speaking (and keeping silent) *means*; that this *'meaning'* of speaking and listening reveals beneath the innocence of speech and hearing the culpable depth of a second *quite different* discourse, the discourse of the unconscious (Althusser: 1968).

Since Althusser wrote this in 1968 in *Reading Capital*, claims and counterclaims for the significance of psychoanalysis have been a familiar part of theoretical writing on socialism and feminism. The idea was revived among Marxists that Freudian ideas could contribute importantly to understanding the social construction of identity. Psychoanalysis was seen, therefore, as a useful tool for investigating the level of ideological representations and their hold on individuals. Some Marxists took this argument further, suggesting that identity as described by Freud was only a precarious construct. The possibilities opened up by this approach were also recognised within feminism. The combined emphasis within psychoanalysis on the unconscious and on infantile sexuality was seen as enormously useful. Psychoanalysis appeared to provide an account of the construction of sexual identity within a patriarchal society. At the same time this identity was not seen as fixed and final, but an identity which is only ever precariously achieved. Thus psychoanalysis seemed to suggest that identity and conscious choice could be both understood and changed.

What is the second discourse which Althusser and many others saw as so significant? It is the material in which the practice of analysis intervenes, the unconscious. The claim made by psychoanalysis is that what is spoken what is exchanged in everyday forms of speech and behaviour and in systems of representation within society, are only half the story. Conscious behaviour, thought and expressions are only the tip of an iceberg. They are compromises formed between unconscious desires and social necessities.

The analytic activity listens to all these representations and behaviours which reveal the workings of the unconscious. These are not seen as activities of some other self but as wishes, fears and desires crucially related to those conscious parts of our behaviour. Certain moments have been isolated by psychoanalytic practice as giving privileged insight into what Freud called that paradoxical activity, unconscious thought. Dreams, jokes, slips of the tongue, forms of 'obsessional', 'ritual' or 'repetitive' behaviour are all held to be moments where unconscious 'meanings' find forms of expression. The metaphor often used is that of a sheet of paper with writing on both sides. Held up to the light, the writing on the other side is seen through the paper. In the case of the relations between the unconscious and conscious there is a more structured relation between the two sides. They are mutually interdependent. Conscious behaviour as a compromise between unconscious wishes and fears and social necessity is structured by unconscious preoccupations. Normal and acceptable modes of behaviour are seen to be structured by latent meanings.

Obviously then, psychoanalysis is not just about 'neurotics'. No one individual is exempt from the process of entry into human culture, the process in which the unconscious is formed. And Freud's writings on religion[1] make it clear that dominant social representations and forms of belief, far from being the 'norm' against which sick people are measured, are expressions of the same structure in which neurotic behaviour is formed.

Where these propositions have been taken as having implications for Marxism and Feminism is in their challenge to the idea of each individual having 'given' personal and human capacities which somehow exempt that individual from the effects of the social formation. Psychoanalytic theory was seen as supplying a missing element to Marxism, which would account for the individual level of social structures as an integral part of her/his individual being. This then would account for the deep hold of ideology. Althusser was also interested in extending these propositions about identity, challenging the whole idea of a coherent individual. Freud's hypotheses had demonstrated that identity is precarious. 'I' am no longer a coherent, conscious, rational being. This 'I' is only the product of choices not taken, desires not fulfilled and conflicts not expressed. But these elements are always likely to return, to disturb and surprise.

What we say, how we say it and what we say by our behaviour can be re-assembled. There is a latent meaning to our actions and utterances. There is unconscious thought which is not obvious to our conscious mind but can be reassembled through the work of analysis which would reveal the process of our historical construction. These assertions as to the fragility of consciousness have been important for investigating the relationship between representation and subjectivity. It has been possible to suggest, for example, that there is no such thing as a coherent subject who either originates or simply supports one ideology. Instead, ideologies can be seen as constructing positions of subjectivity necessary to those representations. One individual may be interpellated by a number of different systems of representation.[2]

The Construction of Masculinity and Femininity

So far so good. But the psychoanalytic account delivers a very specific version of the historical construction of the subject. Its explanation of how conscious and unconscious structures are formed entails a particular account of sexual construction. It is here that the promise and problems of psychoanalysis have been argued for feminism. Particularly under the inspiration of Juliet Mitchell's *Psychoanalysis and Feminism* (Mitchell: 1974) some feminists thought that the critique of constitutioned subjectivity had important implications for feminism. Not only was it possible to displace the idea of a 'given' identity – a presupposition fundamental to sexist ideologies concerning women's inferiority – but also, turning back to Freud, it was clear that his outline had a great deal to say about the route followed in the construction of femininity. It could therefore illustrate how sexual identification arose and why it has such a hold on the emotional life.

Freud's account of the initial bisexuality and polymorphous perversity of the newborn infant had obvious implications for feminism. He claimed that all new-born children have the same drives and aims, which are only organised into masculine and feminine dispositions as a result of the constraints of society, most importantly those of reproduction. Both sexes have activities broadly organised into oral, anal and phallic phases, and sexuality at this stage is predominantly 'active'. The little girl's active clitoral masturbation is seen as the exact equivalent to the boy's phallic phase. It is only through the intervention of cultural complexes that both boy and girl undergo changes in the aims and activities associated with this phallic phase. Freud suggests that through the intervention of the Oedipus and castration complex, the boy and girl child are forced into predominantly (but precariously) masculine and feminine dispositions. The girl child undergoes changes in both her sexual activity and its aim. Not only does she have to renounce her mother's body for good but, according to the Freudian account, the vagina replaces the clitoris as the primary sexual site. For the boy, the threat of castration entails merely the postponement of the aim of his incestuous early desires. He cannot have his mother but he will be able to have women. A number of different versions and explanations of the Oedipus and castration account have been offered. We are perhaps most familiar with that typified by Juliet Mitchell who explains the necessity for the castration complex not as an unavoidable developmental phase but as a requirement of culture in which the primacy of reproduction entails the rigid enforcement of sexual differentiation. I do not intend to discuss this at length (for a full account see Coward: 1980 and 1982). Whatever debates and disagreements have ensued, at the heart of the account is something which is extremely interesting for feminists: it gives one of the first systematic non-essentialist accounts of the construction of sexual identity. At the same time, it recognises the deep hold which the identity, once acquired, has over our thoughts, actions and desires. In 1910, Freud added a footnote to his *Three Essays on Infantile Sexuality*. He wrote:

... from the point of view of psychoanalysis the exclusive interest felt by men for women is also a problem that needs elucidating and is not a self-evident fact based on an attraction that is ultimately of a chemical nature (Freud, 1910).

In this statement is encapsulated Freud's assertion that heterosexual genital attraction is a construct, acquired only with difficulty and then, often only precariously acquired. For Freud this heterosexual identity is imposed by 'culture' – the apparently universal prohibition on incest is interpreted by Freud as a cultural law by which the child must submit to cultural exigencies and abandon its early incestuous desires.

Psychoanalysis, in other words, has been concerned to explore the construction of forms of sexual disposition, masculinity and femininity. The characteristics traditionally associated with men and women, such as aggressivity and passivity, are seen by Freud to be impositions on the anatomical male and female through the intervention of cultural complexes. Moreover the attraction to the opposite sex is acquired with difficulty for the girl child, a perspective which has already been pursued by Luce Irigaray. She argues that the girl child is in compulsory exile from women's body through the imposition of heterosexual reproductive sexuality. Finally, in Freud's account there is no hard and fast division between 'perverted' and 'normal' forms of behaviour. His investigation of the sexual complexes underlying religious representations show how little he was prepared to draw the line between 'neuroses' and acceptable forms of social behaviour.

This is clearly important as it implies there are general cultural imperatives to the manifestation of sexuality. These act on all sexual behaviour from that of the heterosexual couple to that of the rapist. It suggests a way of investigating these links in a way which would seem to bear out feminist insights as to the link between a number of apparently disparate practices.

Representations of women

One area where this approach has already begun to deliver

some returns is in the investigation of cinema and photography from a psychoanalytic point of view. When feminism first investigated these representations, it was a matter of insisting on certain reductive stereotypes. Women seemed to be portrayed in a number of limited and degrading ways – often in mutually exclusive categories: the whore, the sex object, the mother and housewife, etc. While it was necessary to insist on the limited and offensive nature of these categorizations, the investigation of photography and cinema from the perspective of stereotypes was limited in its explanation of why there was such a saturation of images of women in our culture. The analysis of stereotypes concentrated on the content of an image – what was portrayed. There was however another aspect to looking, the question of the pleasure obtained from the act of looking itself. This pleasure clearly involved a general level of cultural fascination with women.

Once studies of the cinema turned to considering not only the 'content' of films but also the structures of pleasure involved in the act of cinematic viewing, it became clear that certain sexual structures, related to the general organization of sexuality in our culture, were implicated. Freudian ideas have again rendered a certain amount of service. For example, it has become possible to detect the fetishistic nature of some images of women which would account for the fragmentation of images of the woman's body in a way rarely found in men. This perspective is clearly not confined to the cinema. It begins to suggest why so much of women's identity is tied up with wanting to be the object of the male look, and why images which might appear to be exclusively addressed to men are fascinating to women too.

The importation of psychoanalytic ideas into the investigation of images has made possible the investigation of the forms and functioning of representations women within the general organization of sexual structures in this society. This approach has been able to reveal the profound ambivalence in many images of women, an ambivalence which indicates the thin line between 'normal' sexual engagement and the violence and antagonism which is so often represented as something exhibited only by 'sick' men.

All these ideas have implications for the discussions on sexuality outlined earlier. They point to the way in which we can explore sexual practices, but without reducing them to the conscious intentions of an anatomical group. They point to ways of investigating what is at stake in the sex act and its relation to other expressions of sexuality. At the same time, they leave us with the problem of investigating how anatomical distinction becomes so significant if masculine and feminine identity cannot be assumed.

These brief comments are not offered as a full account of Freud's thought nor of the numerous and different ways in which his ideas about sexuality have been contested or developed. They are offered here simply to indicate certain propositions arising from psychoanalytic thought which could be considered useful for current investigations of sexuality. Of crucial importance is the irreducibility of the unconscious, with all that this implies for how we understand 'personality', 'identity', 'motivation', etc. Freud's ideas do make it very clear that we are dealing neither with subjects who simply 'copy' cultural roles, nor with individuals who are born with certain definite interests and aspirations. His writings on the unconscious indicate the extent of the problem confronting feminism, the profound way in which our actions and behaviours are structured. But they also indicate that these actions and behaviour can be challenged and changed. Moreover psychoanalytic ideas point to the structuring of masculinity and femininity under the imperative towards heterosexuality, and the centrality of anatomical distinction in our culture. Many critics object to this because of its apparently universalising and therefore pessimistic implications. There obviously are very real problems with the level of generalization about Freud's arguments where the universality of family structures has been confused with the universality of psychic structuring. However, the psychoanalytic account does suggest a way to dissect the forms of subjectivity produced for us in cultural formations.

Psychoanalysis: theory and practice

Given that I am making wide claims for psychoanalysis's

insight into the cultural representations of sexuality, it might be asked why it is that psychoanalysis is far from an accepted theoretical approach within the movement. Leaving aside outright rejection of Freud as an ideologue of patriarchy, psychoanalysis still has a controversial place within the movement.

Many feminists feel that the implications of psychoanalysis for Women's Liberation have got lost under the weight of theoretical argument. One might be forgiven for taking this view. The edge of feminist interest has been taken off by its transformation into a theoretical tool against the appearance of essentialism or reductionism in any discourse. Necessary though such a pursuit might have been, and I personally think it was, it now seems to have become an end in itself, rather than a first step in developing a theoretical problematic appropriate to and adequate for feminist politics. Also, this general level of debate about psychoanalysis has tended to obscure the ways in which it had been productively applied and also its continuing tradition as a mode of enquiry into female sexuality.

This obscuring underlies a further complaint from feminists: namely, that psychoanalysis is all future promise. Many who are familiar with the broad claims made for psychoanalysis feel that they have yet to be substantiated. This is in part an effect of the dual role of psychoanalysis on the one hand as a practice, on the other as a theory. Criticism against both for their mystificatory perpetuation of the patriarchal status quo seem to me misplaced though not entirely without foundation. At the level of practice, feminists tend to have a range of contradictory responses – those who turn to therapy but treat it as entirely personal with no implications for their theoretical or political work; those who guard psychoanalysis as an inviolate profession to be defended against feminist 'corruption'; those who regard the practice of psychoanalysis as something only available to rich and idle women; those who see its damaging effects as practised in the psychologization of social problems in areas such as social work; finally those who regard the interest in psychoanalytical theory as something which ultimately leads us inwards, into ourselves and away from political and public engagement.

All these reservations are worth treating seriously, but often

the true object of criticism is neither the theoretical
foundations of psychoanalysis, nor indeed the multitude of
ways in which Freudian psychoanalysis has influenced the
various forms of therapy and analysis available. Many of the
stances which some feminists find objectionable do not arise
from anything intrinsic to psychoanalysis, but from other
professional/medical and political stances within our society.

The first point that should be made is that psychoanalysis is
anything but the arm of the state in any simple sense. I would
be much comforted by the idea that any form of mental stress
was treated in the first instance by some form of counselling,
but all evidence is that the lack of resources within the NHS
and the dominance of bio-chemical explanations within
medicine mean that therapy/counselling and analysis do in
fact remain at the margins – privately-financed institutions,
loosely affiliated groups like the Women's Therapy Centre,
with only limited availability in psychiatric wards. All
underfinanced and oversubscribed, some attempting means
testing to expend their constituency, none could be called the
approved ideologues of the state. What's more, orthodox
psychoanalysis now, as it did when first championed by
Freud, still constitutes a challenge to dominant means of
classifying mental problems and psychological states. Patients
may not be treated as constitutional 'criminals',
'homosexuals' or whatever in quite such a crude way.
However, although many psychoanalytic tenets have passed
into a sort of popular knowledge, it is still true that
psychoanalytic notions of the unconscious and the complexity
of motive and identity are hardly represented in the most
usual ways of treating mental illness.

The charge that psychoanalysis is patriarchal both in
theory and practice is also sustained only with difficulty. For
one thing, the practice and theory of psychoanalysis is
strangely dominated by women, in a way rarely paralleled by
other 'professions'. One could offer a number of hypotheses
about this phenomena. There is the absence of formal medical
qualifications, the attraction to Jungian archetypes and quite
traditional notions of the sex roles. Whatever the reason for
their presence, which may be quite conservative, the *effect* of it
has been to guarantee the continual investigation of female

sexuality. The fruitful direction pursued by Irigaray (1977), superficially appearing to be a thorough critique of Freud, is only a continuation of a long tradition of women analysts engaged in the practice and production of psychoanalytic theory adequate to the female experience.

The charge of conservative effects of psychoanalysis is perhaps more difficult to prove or disprove. The suggestions made that psychoanalysis is used within social work as a prop for a view of the normal, heterosexual reproductive family may again not be entirely attributable to psychoanalysis, but to the fact that a definite ideology of and coercive intervention in the family have mobilised aspects of psychoanalysis to provide some crude psychological account of human motives and relations – all basically confined to the nuclear family. Charges against the corrupting 'personal' effects of professional or therapeutic involvements with analysis seems to me even more dubious. Any form of 'professionalism' in our society tends to entail practices which conflict with our projections of a more egalitarian society. And for women, as we know to our cost in many fields, engagement in male professional hierarchies tends to produce all sorts of personal compromises to deal with the contradictions and pressures under which women are placed.

Over and above this, the criticisms against analysis and therapy for leading inwards seem to derive from a misplaced sense of what is truly political. This idea is one that we are all too familiar with in the arenas from which it originates, that is Marxist groups. Here the emphasis is, for strategic reasons, on the need to deal with the structural conditions of inequality rather than assuming that oppressions encountered by individuals or groups derive from themselves rather than the distribution of wealth and power. We have learnt in the Women's Movement that there is everything to be said about so-called internal structures. If there is to be any investigation of female sexuality, its coercion into reproduction through heterosexual relationships, the pleasures and possibilities of our engagement with both sexes, the investigation of our past, our histories, the detailing of our complex engagement in the world *can never* be something irrelevant. Any position which could suggest that to be the case can only diminish what we are, and underestimate our potential for change.

Conclusion

As both theory and therapeutic practice, psychoanalysis is crossed by dominant attitudes of 'professionalism' within this society. Many of the criticisms directed at the content of psychoanalysis would perhaps be more usefully turned against the patriarchal hierarchies within educational and medical establishments which seek to reinforce and maintain social divisions. As such it would be utopian to assume that the theory could be liberated to provide a number of 'solutions' to the political problems encountered by feminism. Like any theory it can have a necessary but not direct relation to politics. Theory can be mobilised in response to political developments; its mobilisation can even determine what those political directions can be. But to assume that any theory could provide all political answers would be falling into the dogmatism which feminists have often had to oppose within Marxism. Furthermore, psychoanalysis has nothing to say about the workings of the state, the economy and politics as they are traditionally conceived. It is a theory and practice which has implications for how these are thought, but it is not an alternative political dogma. Our discussions of sexuality must be developed, not just in themselves, but in a way that displaces these traditional notions of the political. Some propositions from psychoanalysis still have much to teach us.

This article is based on a paper presented to the Communist University of London in 1980 and rewritten in the light of discussions with the Socialist Feminist Social Policy Group: Fran Bennett, Maria Black, Wendy Clark, Rosa Heys, Sue Lawrence, Margaret Page, Ann Wickham. The ideas have subsequently been developed in 'Linguistic, Social and Sexual Relations', *Screen Education*, Summer 1981, no. 39 (with Maria Black) and in *Patriarchal Precedents* (1982).

References

1. These include *Moses and Monotheism* (1939), *The Future of an Illusion* (1927) and *Totem and Taboo* (1912).
2. For a more detailed account of the concepts of *interpellation* and representation, see Althusser, Louis, 'Ideology and Ideological State Apparatuses', in *Lenin and Philosophy* (1971. The concepts are further developed by Paul Q. Hirst, in 'Althusser and the theory of Ideology', in *Economy and Society* vol. 5, No. 4 (1976).

Bibliography

Althusser, Louis, *Reading Capital* (1968).

Black, M., and Coward, R., 'Linguistic, Social and Sexual Relations', *Screen Education*, Summer 1981, no. 39.

Coward, Rosalind, 'On the Universality of the Oedipus Complex', in *Critique of Anthropology*, (Spring 1980), Vol 4, No. 15.

Coward, R., *Patriarchal Precedents* (1982).

Freud, Sigmund, *Three Essays on Infantile Sexuality* (1910) in *Penguin Freud Library*, Vol 7, *On Sexuality* (1977).

Irigaray, Luce, 'Women's Exile: Interview with Luce Irigaray', in *Ideology and Consciousness* No. 1. (1977).

Mitchell, Juliet, *Psychoanalysis and Feminism* (1974).

Notes on Contributors

Michèle Barrett teaches sociology at the City University, London. She is the author of many articles on feminism and has recently published *Women's Oppression Today: Problems in Marxist Feminist Analysis*, (Verso/NLB, 1980). She is a member of the *Feminist Review* Collective.

Rosalind Brunt teaches Communication Studies at Sheffield City Polytechnic. She co-edited, with George Bridges, *Silver Linings: Some Strategies for the Eighties* (Lawrence & Wishart, 1981).

Rosalind Coward lectures in Visual Communications at Goldsmiths College, London. She is a non-aligned socialist feminist and has contributed articles on a range of issues to *Spare Rib, Feminist Review* and to specialist journals, including *Screen* and *Critique of Anthropology*. She co-authored, with John Ellis, *Language and Materialism* (RKP, 1977).

Tricia Davis is coordinator of the Birmingham Trade Union Resource Centre. She is also doing research on Women in the Communist Party (1945-60) at the Centre for Contemporary Cultural Studies, Birmingham University. She has written articles for a range of journals, including *Feminist Review* and *Marxism Today*, and also contributed to several books on different aspects of feminism. She has two children and is active in Birmingham Women's Liberation and the Communist Party.

Florence Keyworth is a journalist at the *Morning Star* and writes frequently for the Women's Page. She has been a member of the Communist Party since 1938 and joined the staff of the *Daily Worker* in 1945.

Mary McIntosh teaches sociology at the University of Essex. She has been active in the women's movement since 1970 and has published articles on sexuality and on feminism and social policy. She is a member of the *Feminist Review* Collective.

Caroline Rowan teaches in adult education institutes in London. She is also doing research on state intervention and the family at the Centre for Contemporary Cultural Studies, Birmingham, and working on a book on the transformation of the British state, 1880-1930, with the CCCS State group.

Sonja Ruehl works at the Open University, and has been involved in the interdisciplinary course 'The Changing Experience of Women', which starts in 1983. She had been active in the women's and gay movement and reviewed books and films for *Gay News*. She is a member of the *Feminist Review* Collective.